I0488357

Jill Scipione

Psalms and Prophets

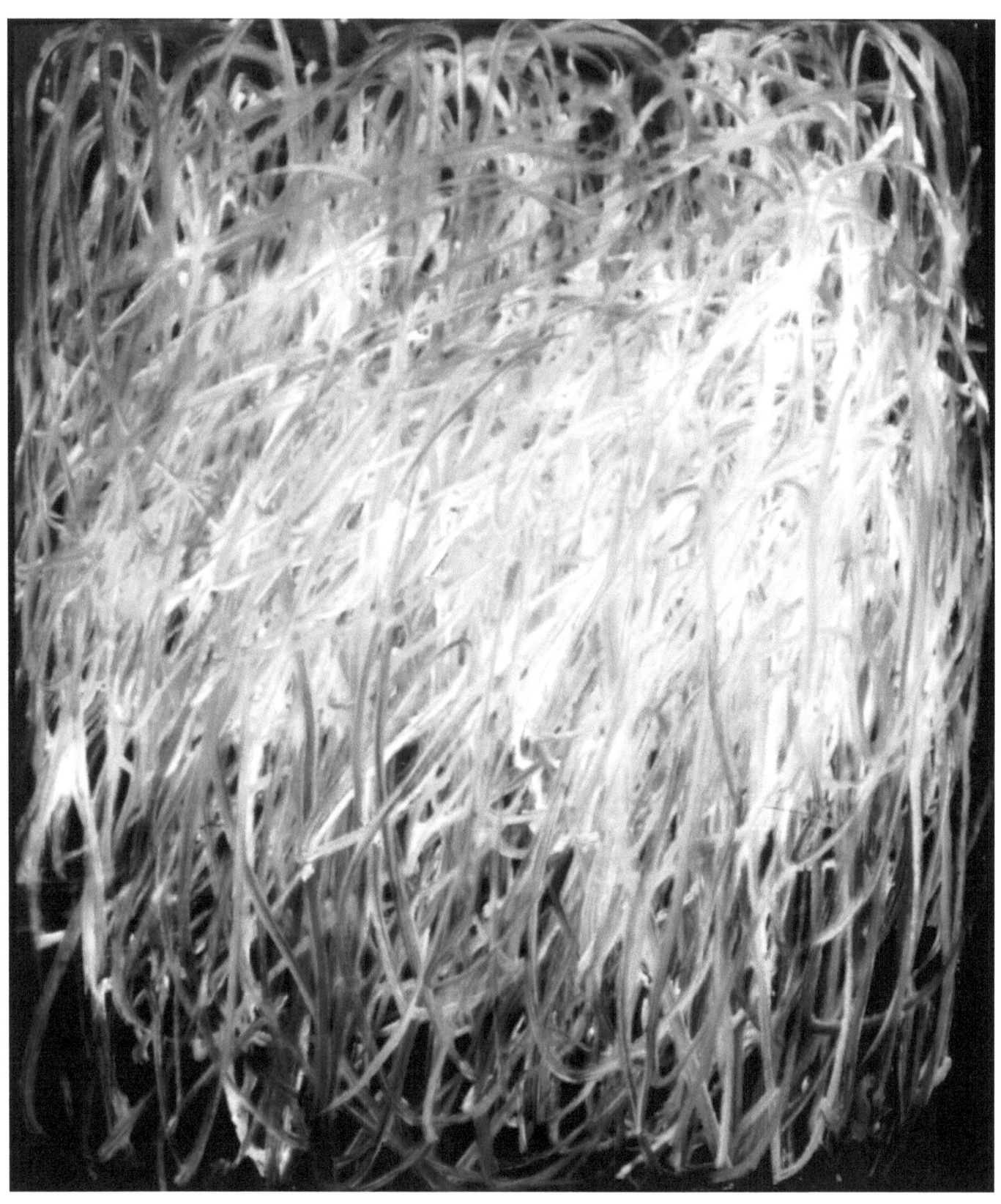

Destruction at Noonday 72" x 60" oil on canvas 1992

Jill Scipione

Psalms and Prophets

DRAWING ROOMS

VICTORY HALL PRESS

In the early 1990s, Jill Scipione began a series of works with the intent of creating a space descriptive of concepts from passages of the Biblical Psalms and Prophets, particularly Isaiah and Ezekiel. These paintings came to be about light traced into dark; her drawing line becoming a painted trail of movement, creating and diffusing figures, forms and atmospheres. Four or five distinct groupings of work emerged, including themes of wheels, vehicles, objects/structures, veils, and eventually a set in which parts of figures from Giotto's early Renaissance paintings are rephrased. The entire series consists of about forty oil on linen or canvas paintings, varying in size from 6 x 5ft to 5 x 4ft with additional smaller works and drawings.

To achieve the dense, physicality of surface that these works required, Scipione used a heavy-bodied oil paint with a stand oil medium to create a tough, visceral stroke. Typically, each work was planned and developed days ahead of when she would enter the studio to paint and then the actual painting came together with great energy and urgency, sometimes in a single day's work - all the aspects having to interact while the surface was wet and malleable. As the series continued, she sometimes introduced other materials: marble dust, fibers and grit into the paint to achieve the textures and surfaces that the works required.

The paintings use white as light; emphatically drawn structures with lines laid over and over another emerge from a deep, dark space created from subtle mixtures of blue and umber. As the works progress, the light pushes forward to meet the viewer as the space behind retreats. Ladders, snares, scaffolds and chariots resolve themselves as temporary forms, consistent with the biblical visions that inspired them, and carrying a weight of meaning and mystery. As the series reaches its climax, forms become clarified. Heavy strokes of white paint coalesce into shrouded figures and illumined shapes borrowed from Giotto's saints and crowds: the clothing of men, women, and angels. The darkness behind solidifies. In the final images, drawn from Psalms and Lamentations, the figures dissolve into line again, but this time more wildly, with colors of earth and flesh mixed in. The darkness becomes the waters into which the soul sinks. Throughout the series there is a dynamic balance that creates excitement; the push and pull of foreground images and deep space, of objects and structures dissolving and forming. At times, the paint itself becomes dimensional and sculptural, almost forming itself into object.

Scipione's subsequent work developed in directions that draw from the concepts she began to explore in these paintings. She later began creating photo-realistic renditions of cuts of meat, at times arranged to comprise forms of wheels and vehicles, and in her most recent pieces, the figurative forms borrowed from the Renaissance are starting to emerge again, this time as densely colored monoliths, hovering in a white vacuum. The images, explorations, mystery and vitality of these earlier paintings became source and symbol for her new works.

I Will Deliver Him 72" x 46" oil on canvas 1992

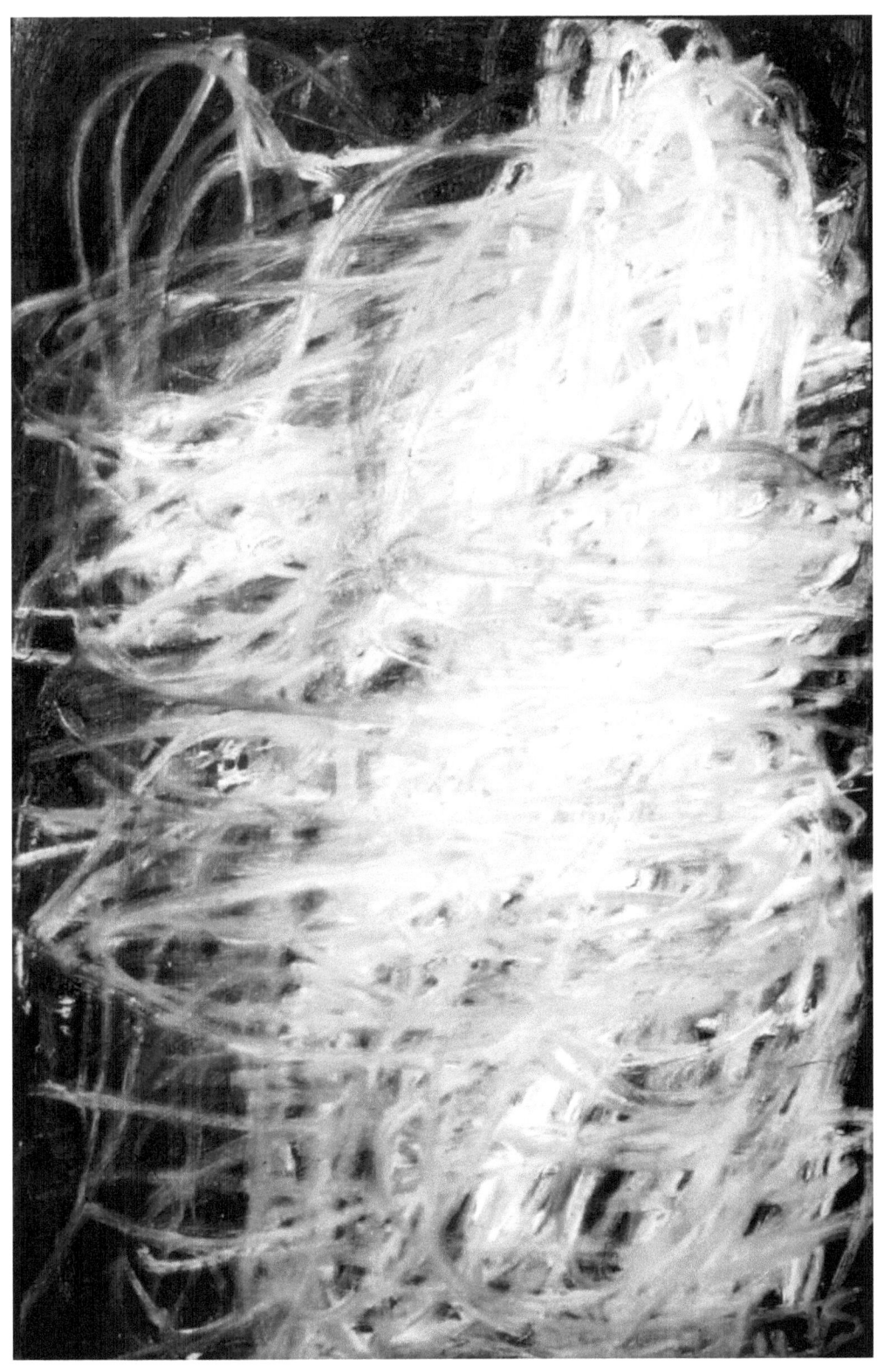

Terror by Night 60" x 48" oil on linen 1992

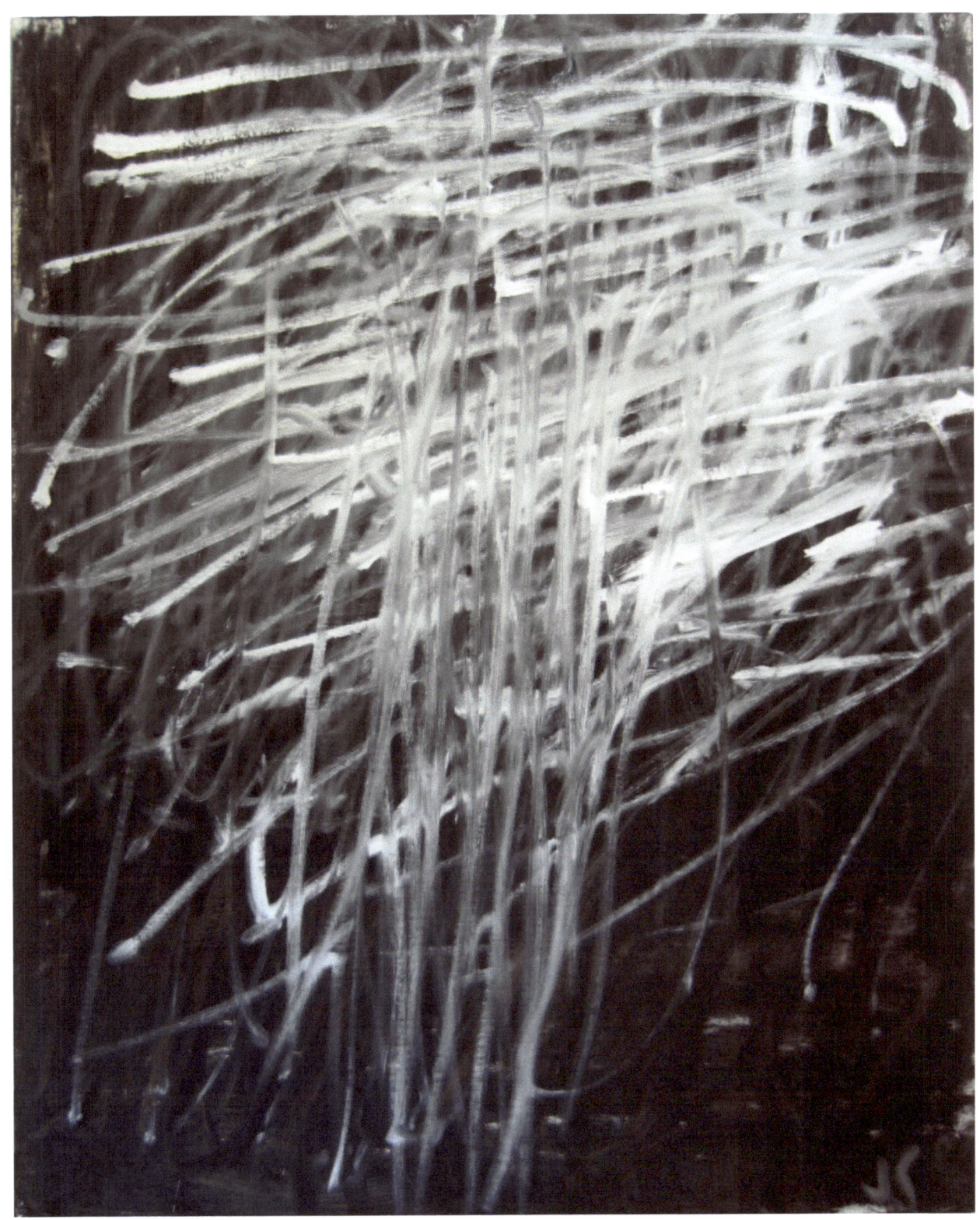

Expanse 60" x 48" oil on canvas 1993

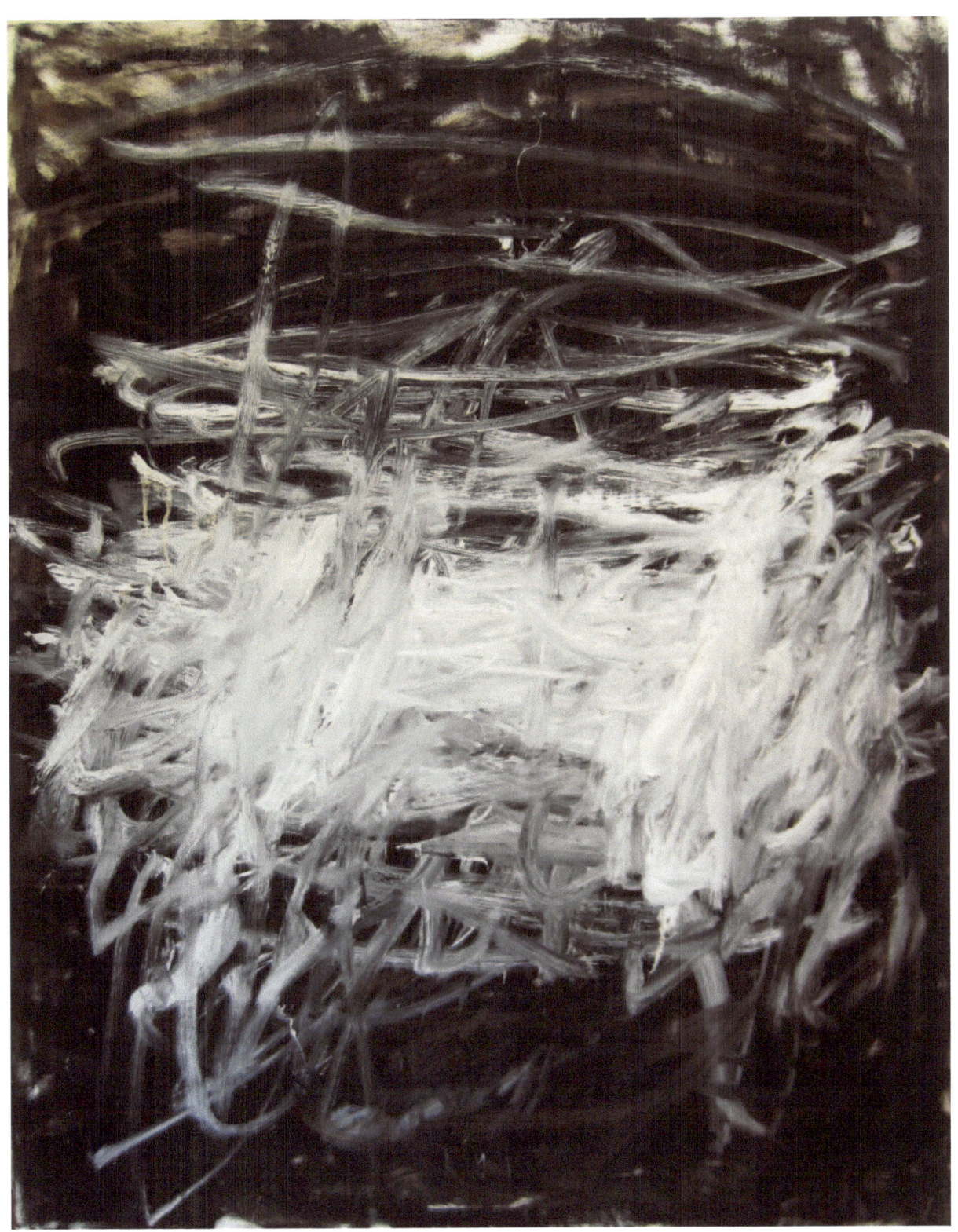

Tent 72" x 48" oil on linen 1992

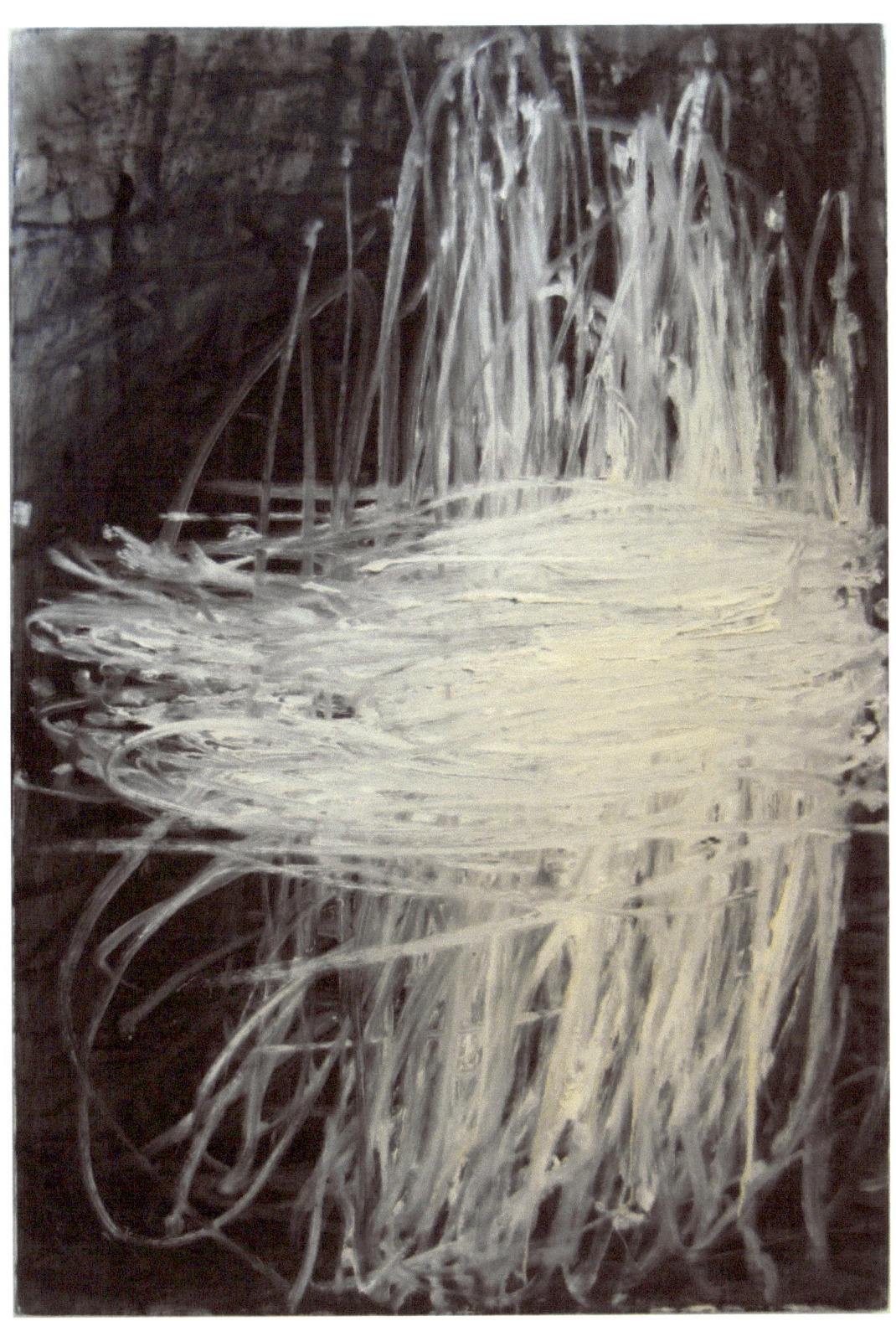

Height 72" x 48" oil on canvas 1993

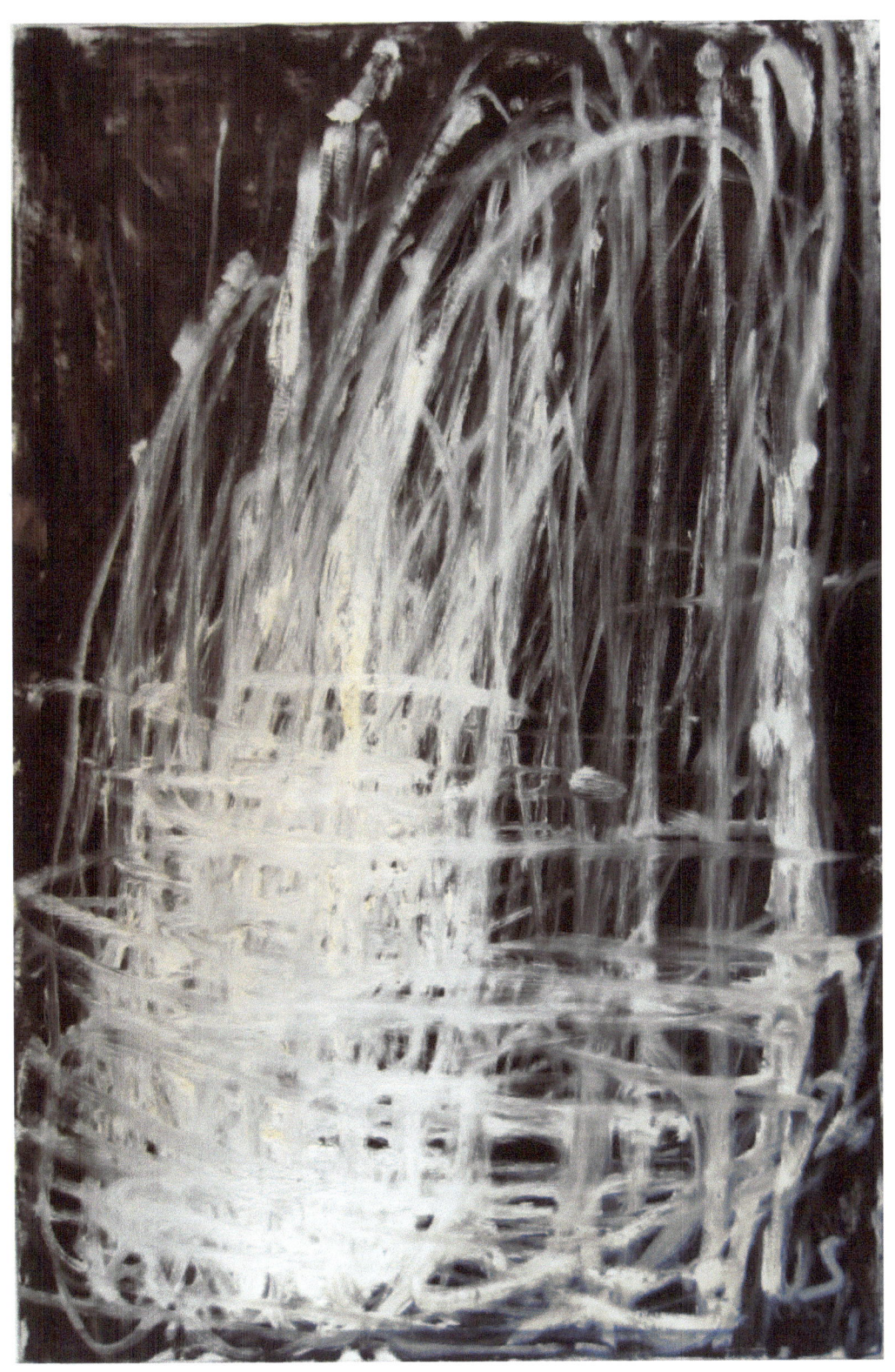

Snare of the Fowler 72" x 48" oil on linen 1993

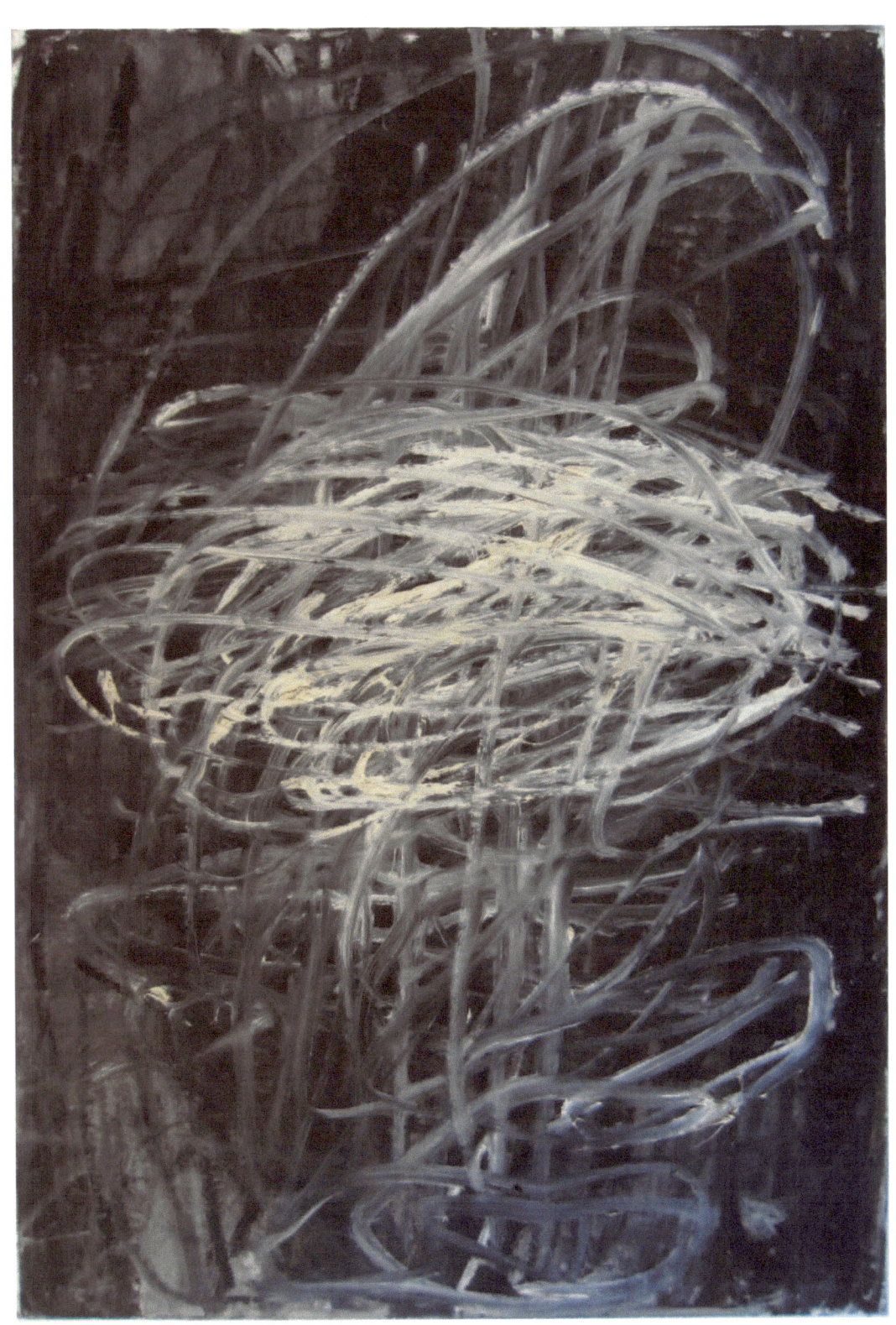

Scaffolding 72" x 48" oil on linen 1993

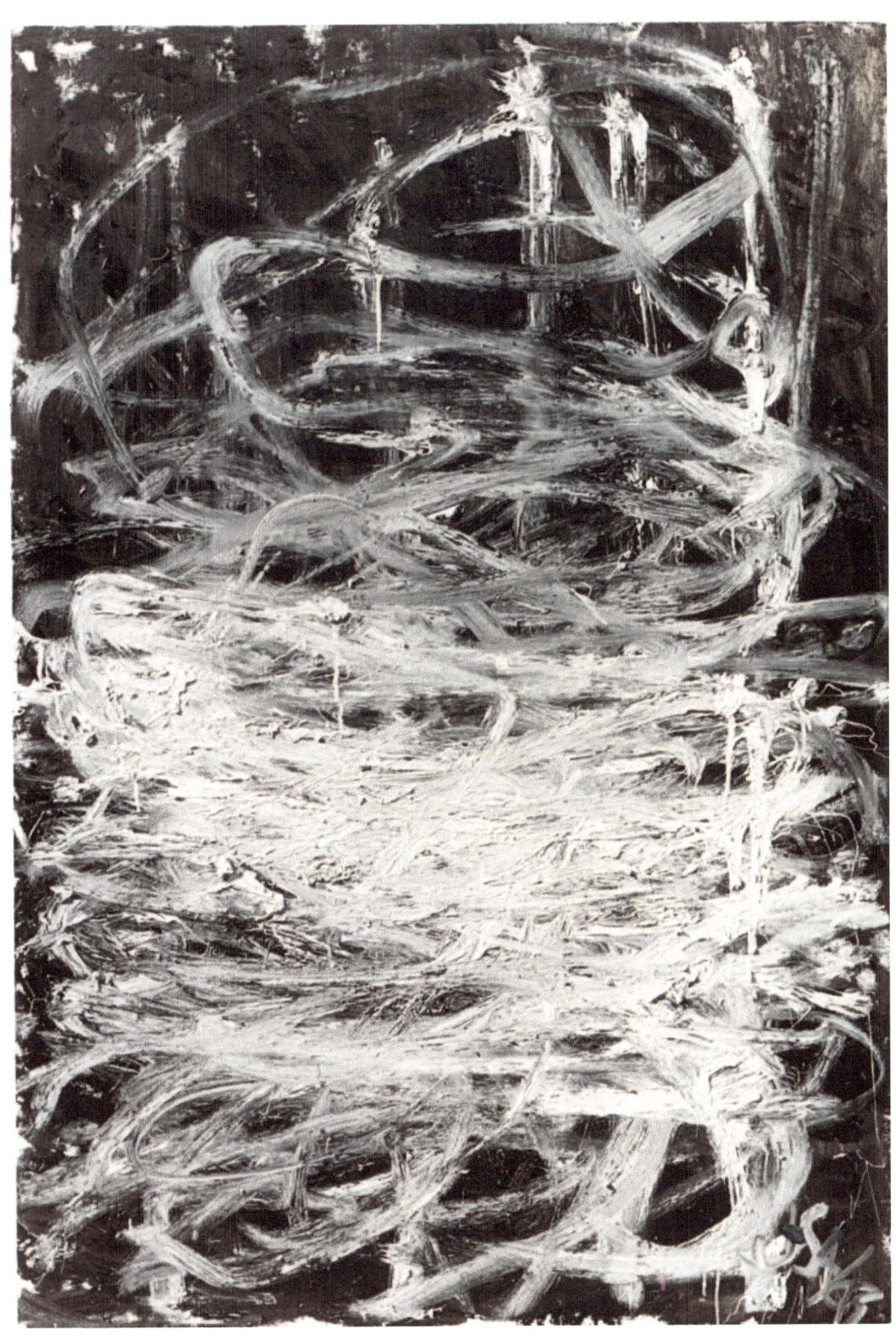

Conveyance 60" x 48" oil on linen 1993

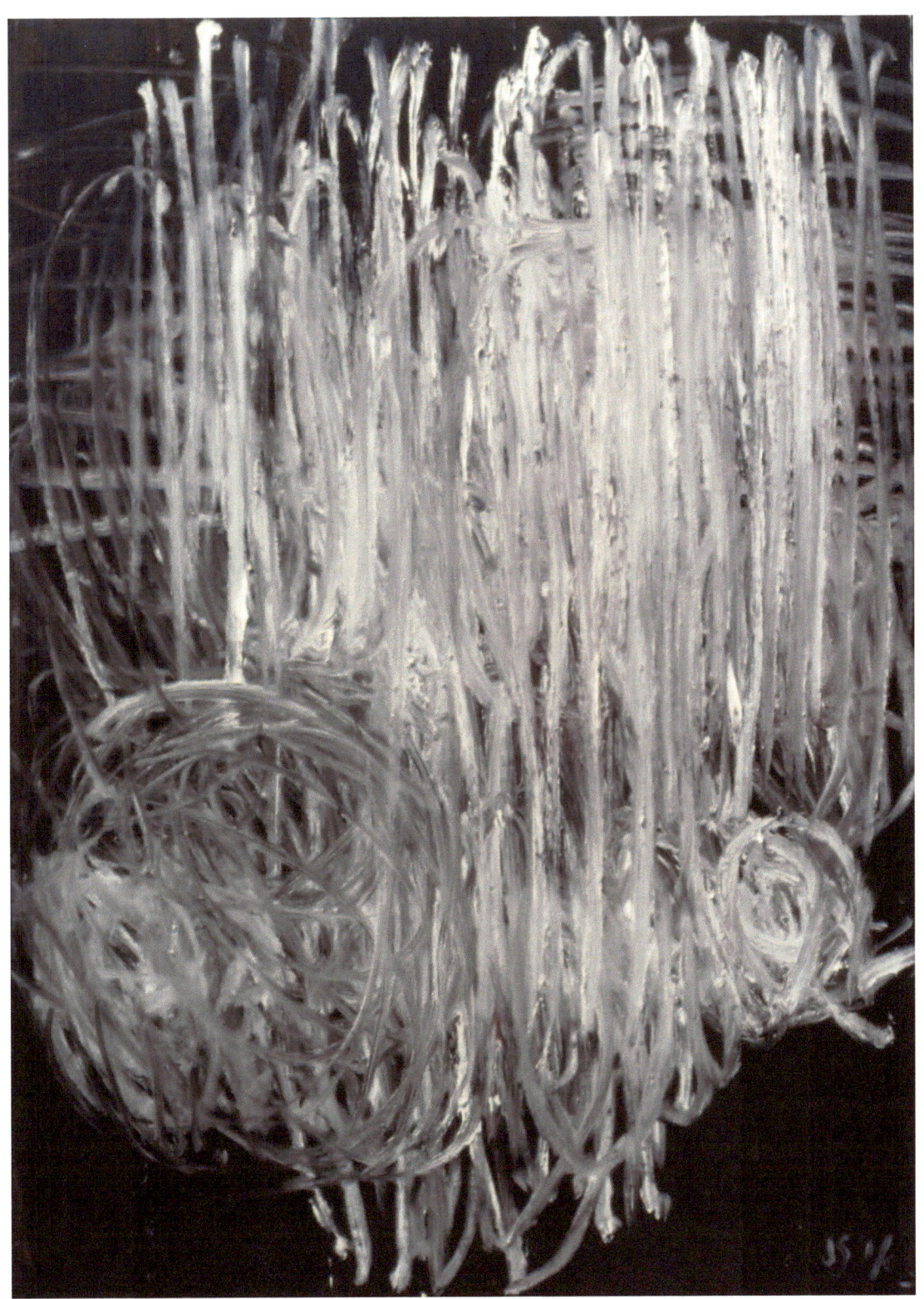

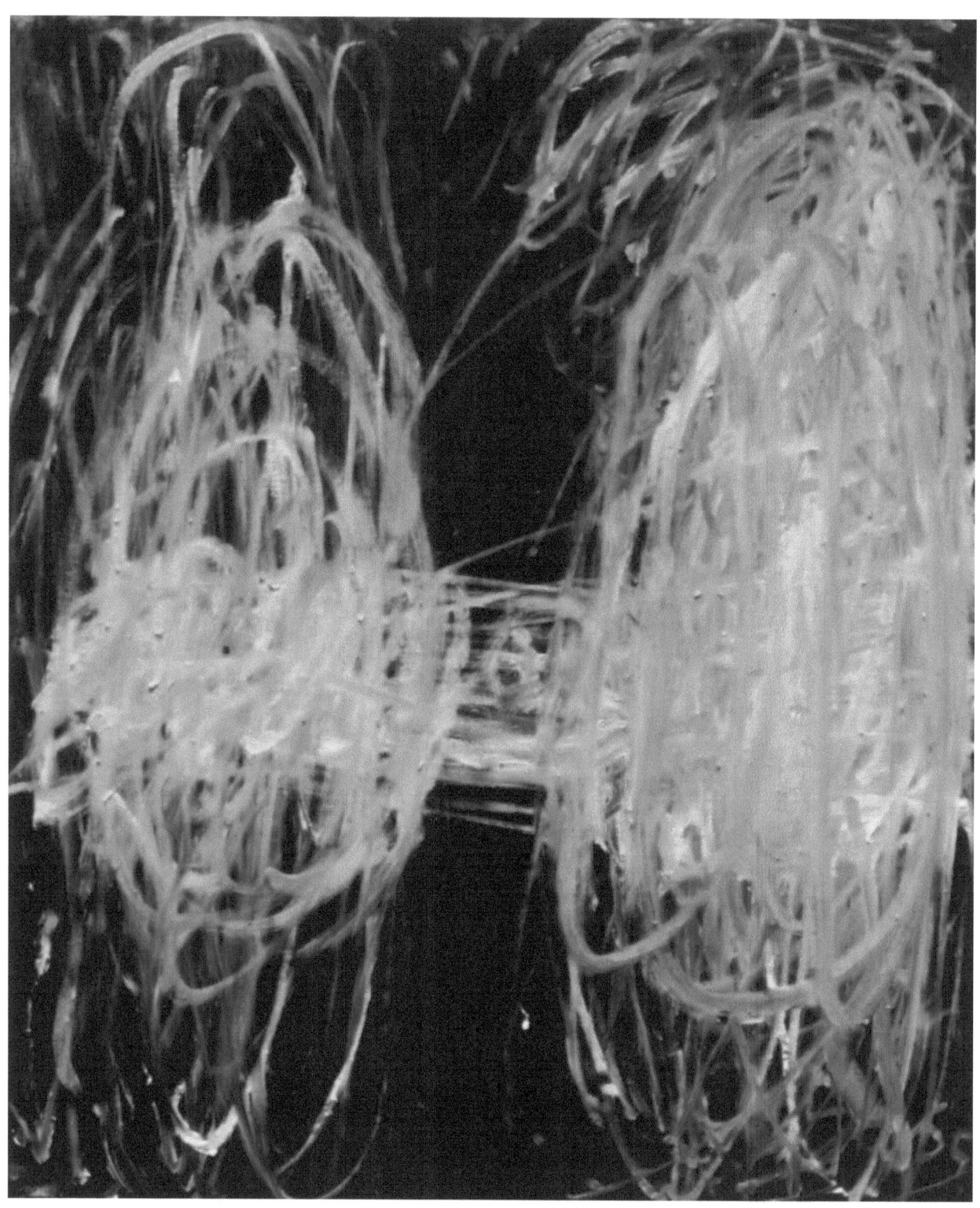

Chariot   72" x 60"   oil on canvas 1993

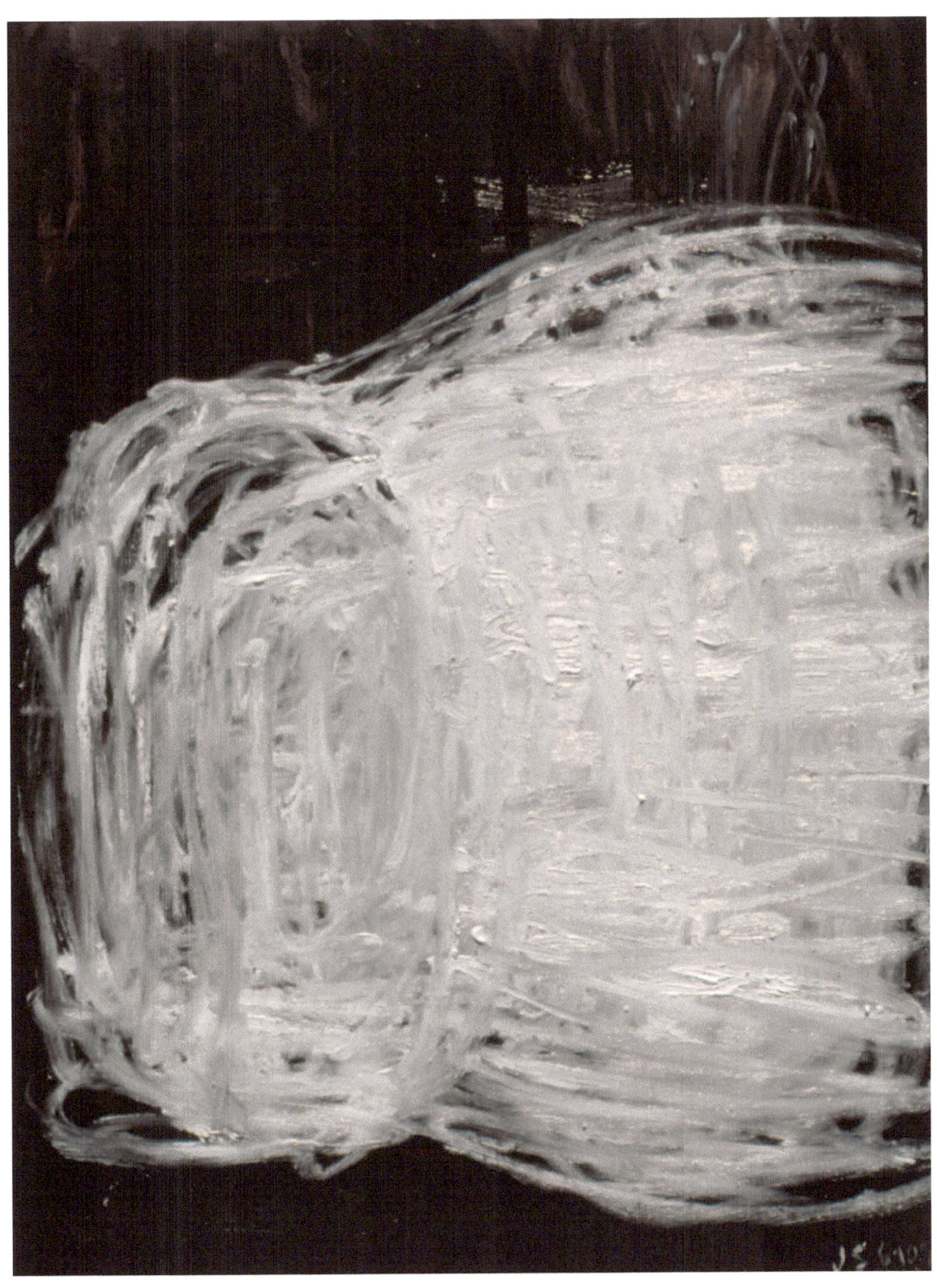

In the Midst of the Wheels 67" x 48" oil on canvas 1993

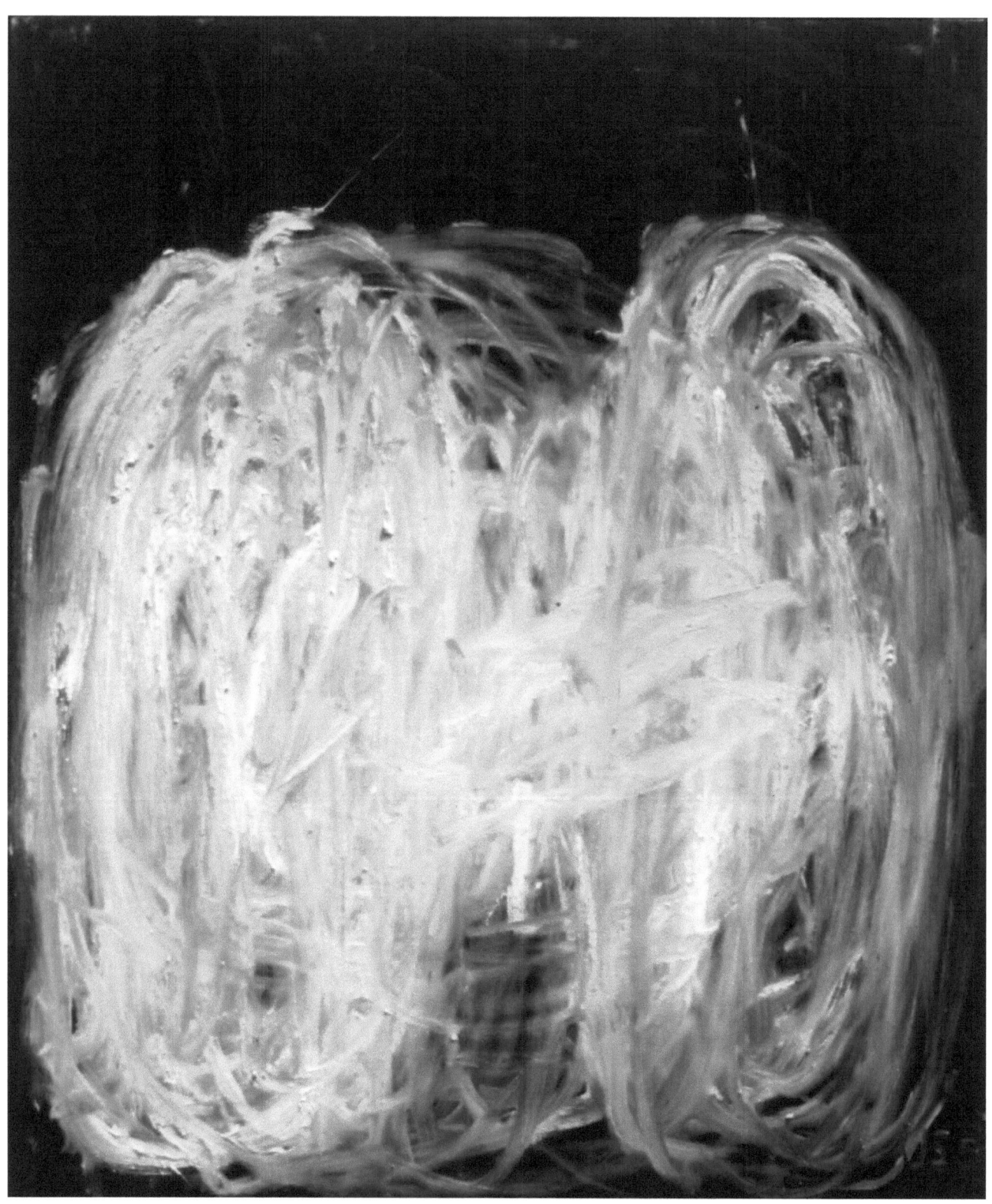

Wheels   72" x 60" oil on canvas 1993

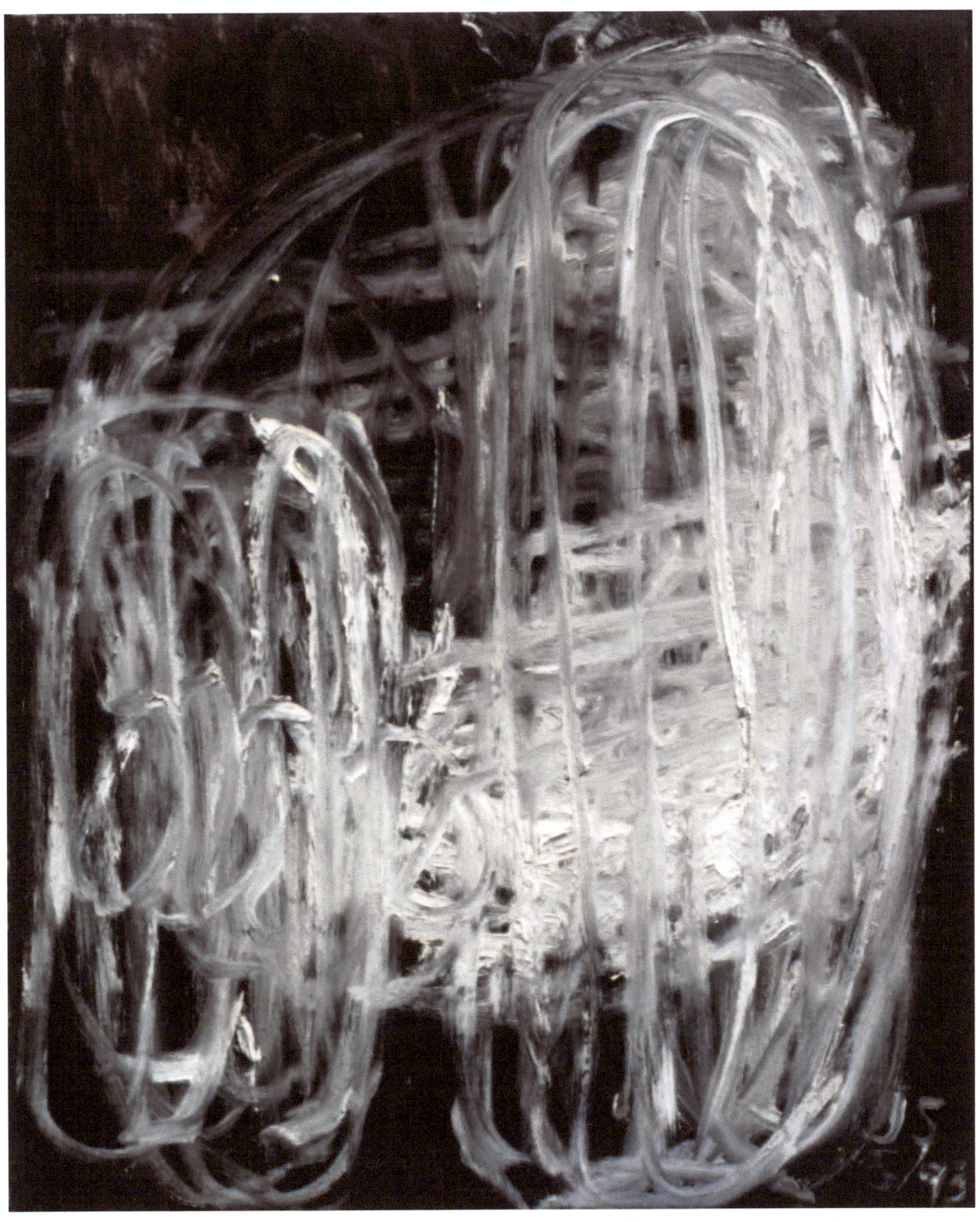

Vehicle   72" x 60"   oil on canvas   1993

Wheel in the Sky, Wheel on the Earth 72" x 48" oil on canvas 1993

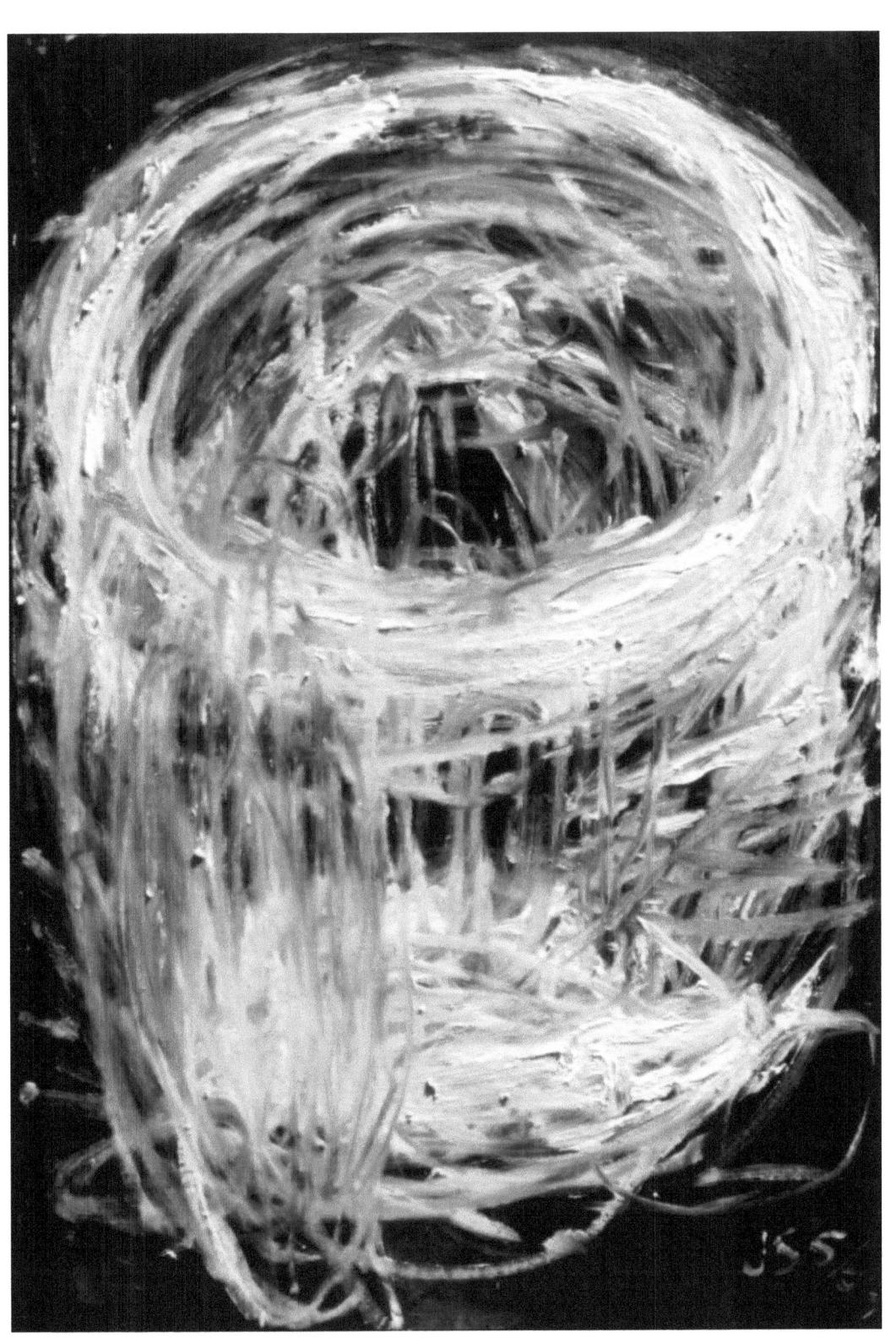

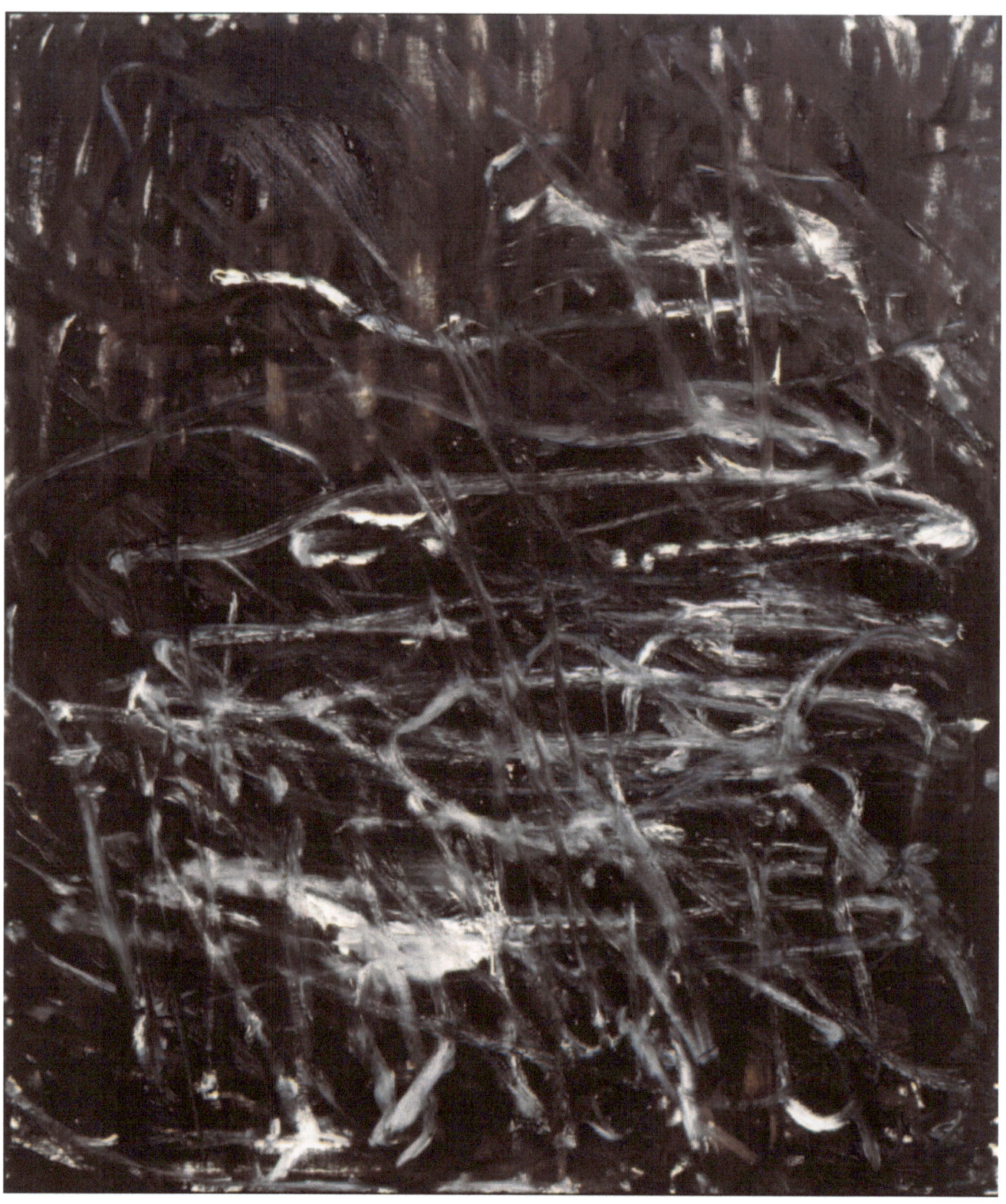

Darkness is not Dark 72" x 60" oil on canvas 1993

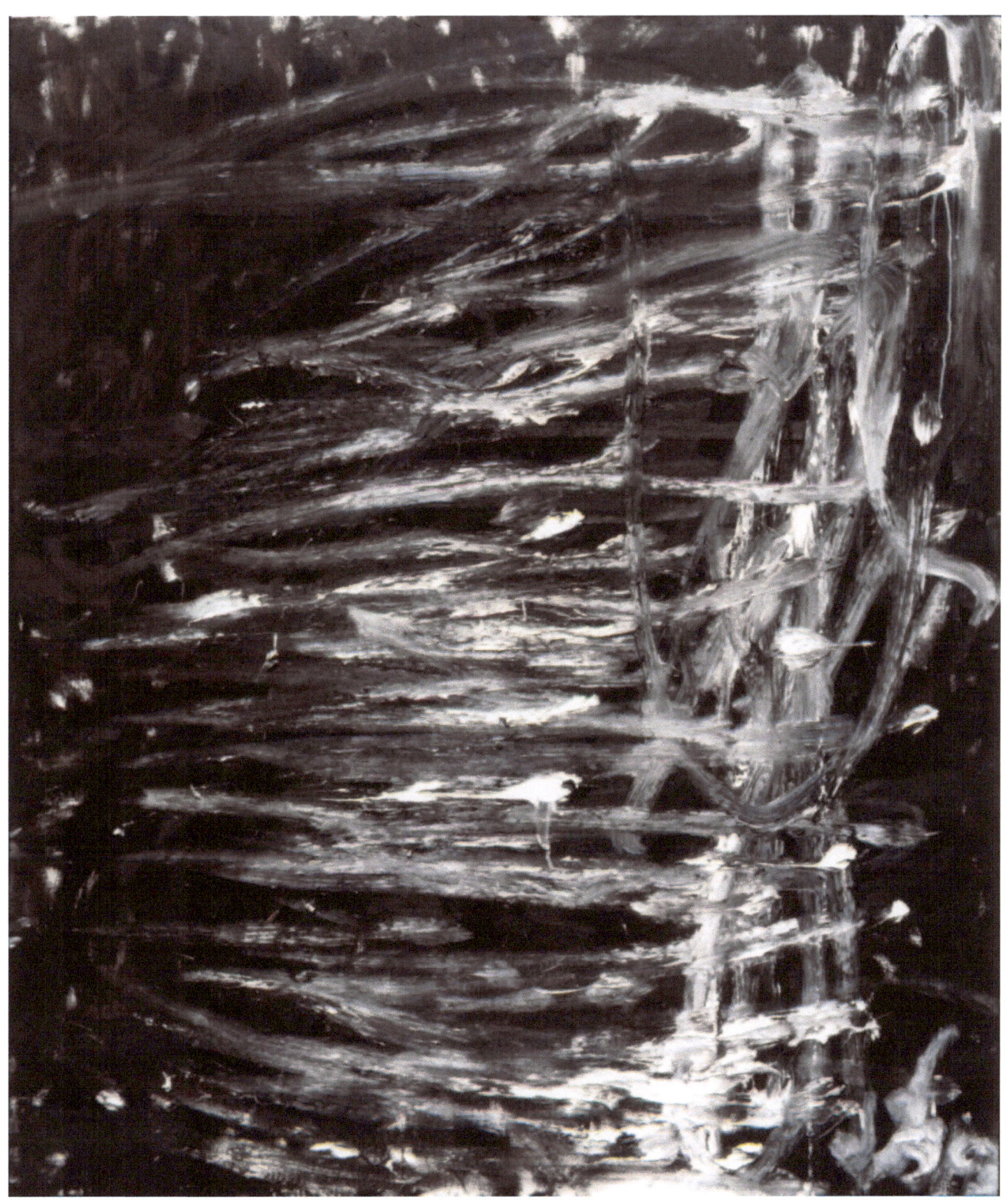

Threshing Instrument with Teeth 72" x 60" oil on canvas 1993

Messenger 72" x 60" oil on canvas 1993

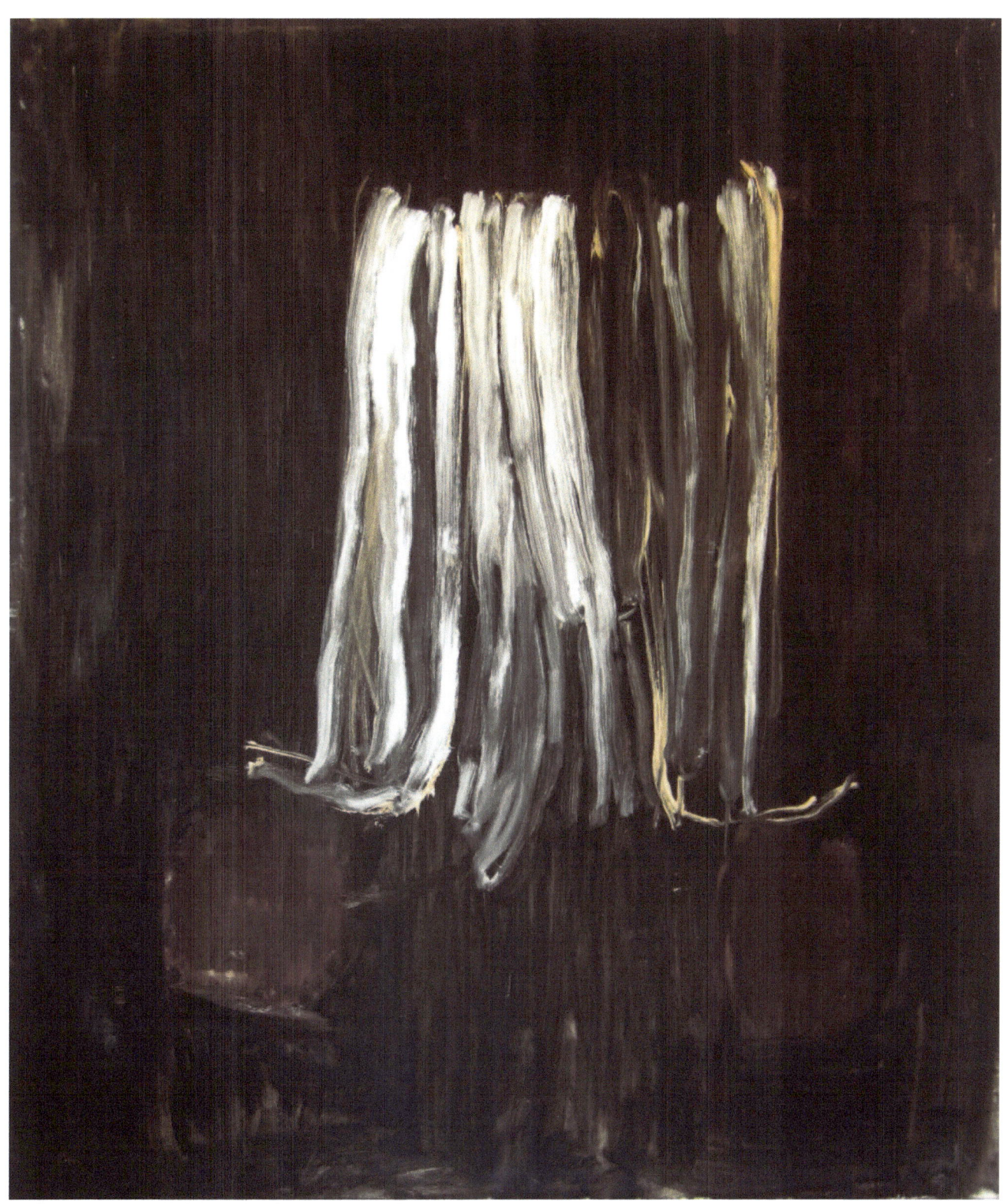

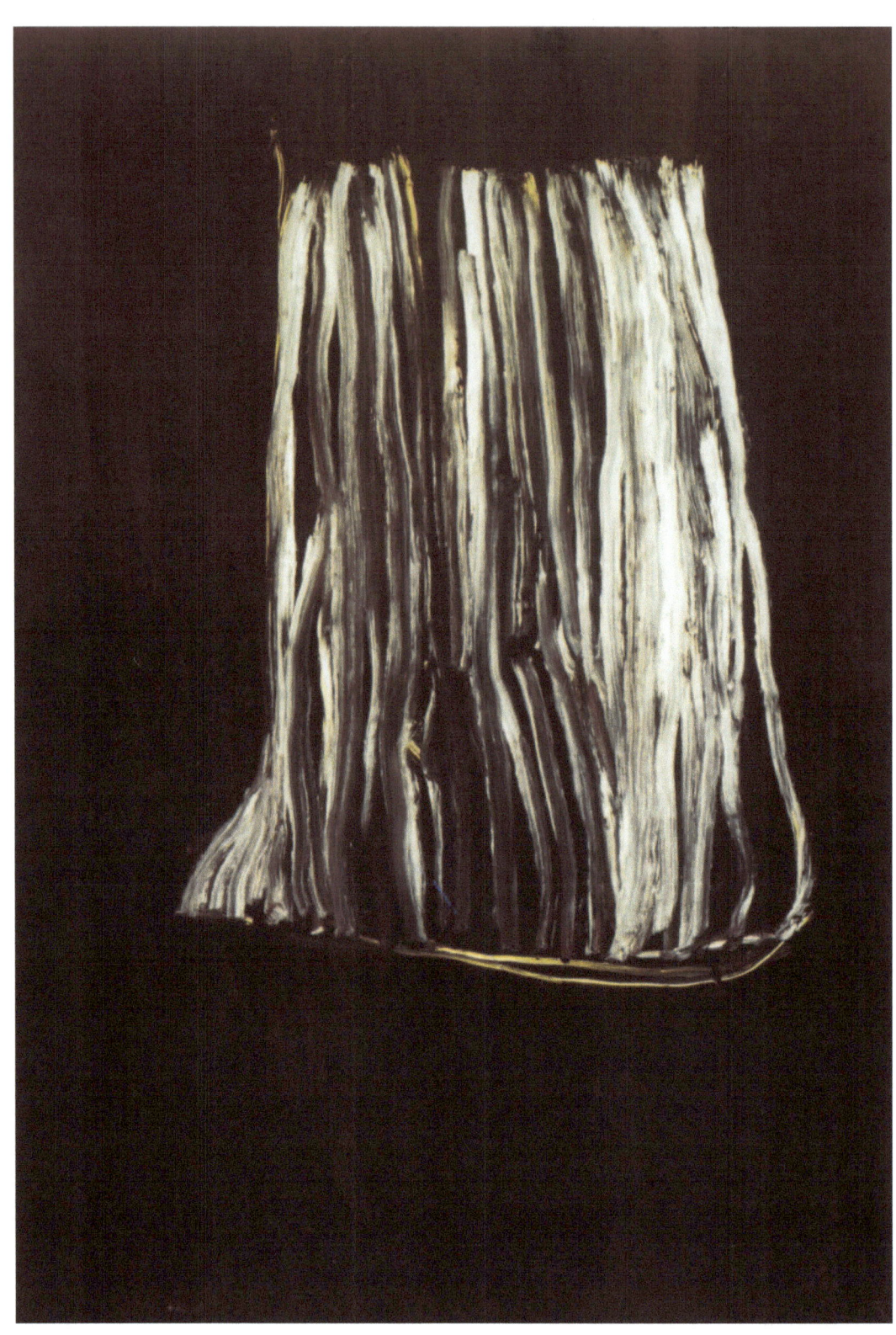

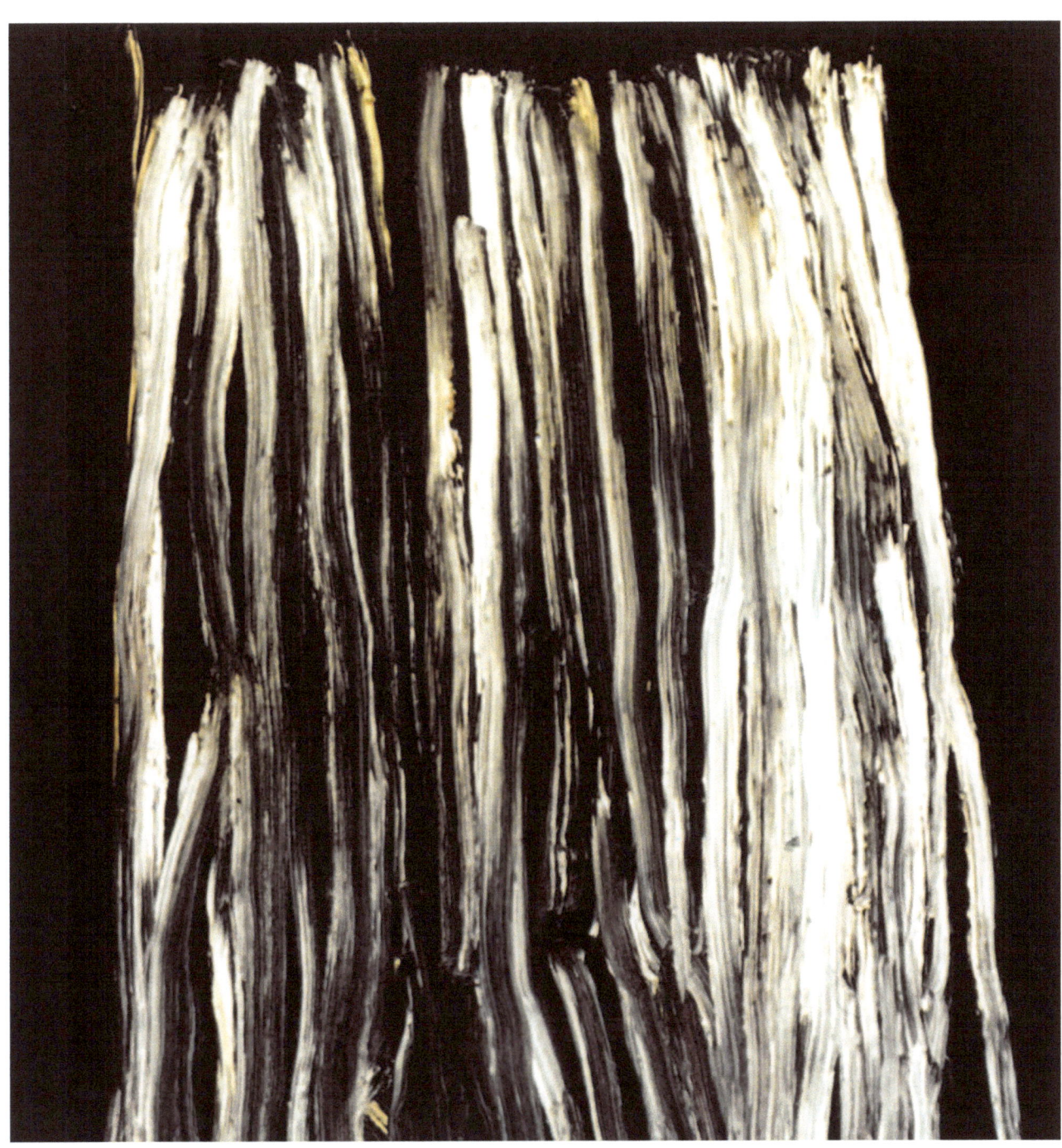

Opposite: Radiant Being 72" x 48" oil on canvas 1993
Above: detail

Servant 72" x 48" oil on canvas   1993

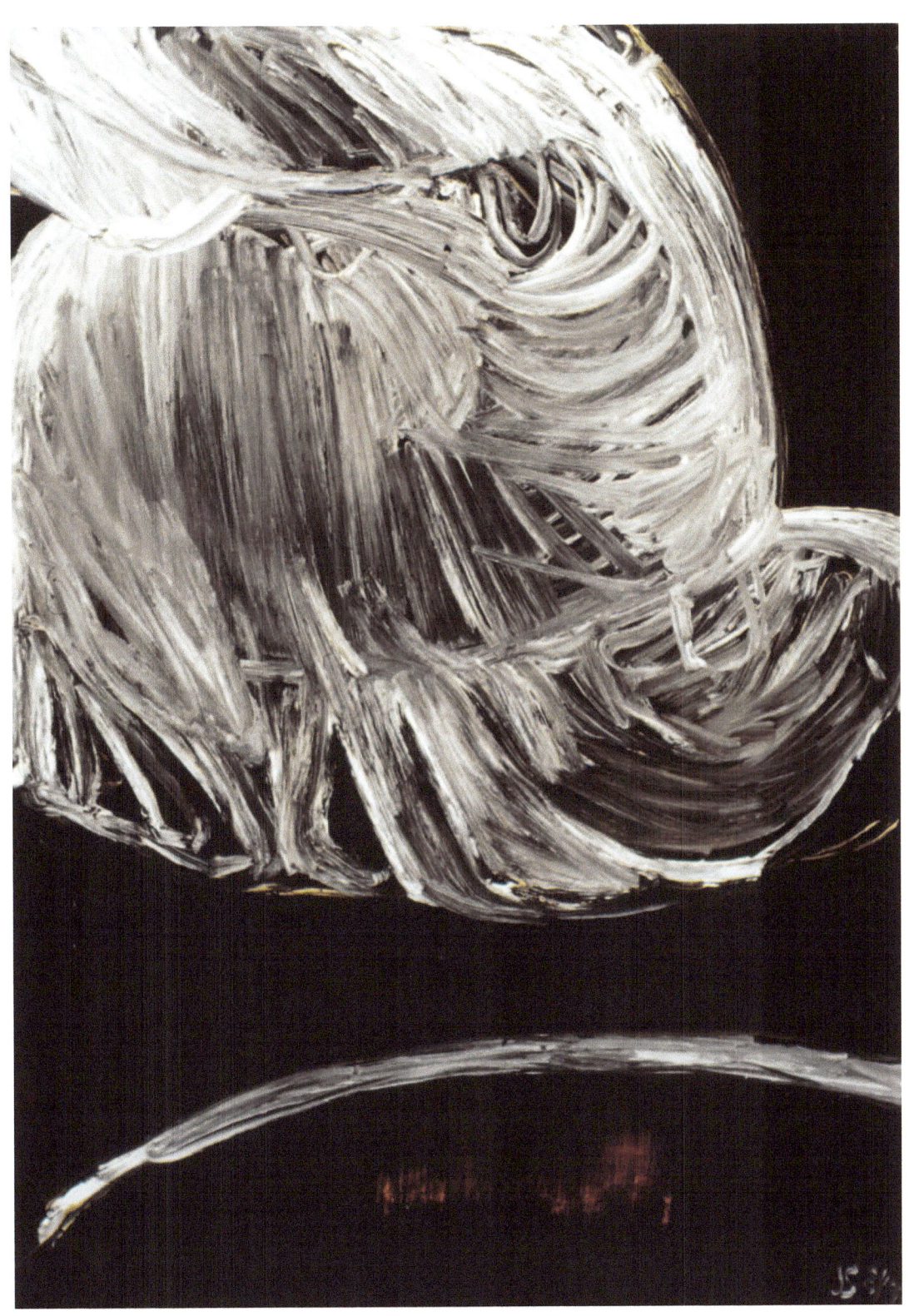

Magi   72" x 48" oil on canvas 1993

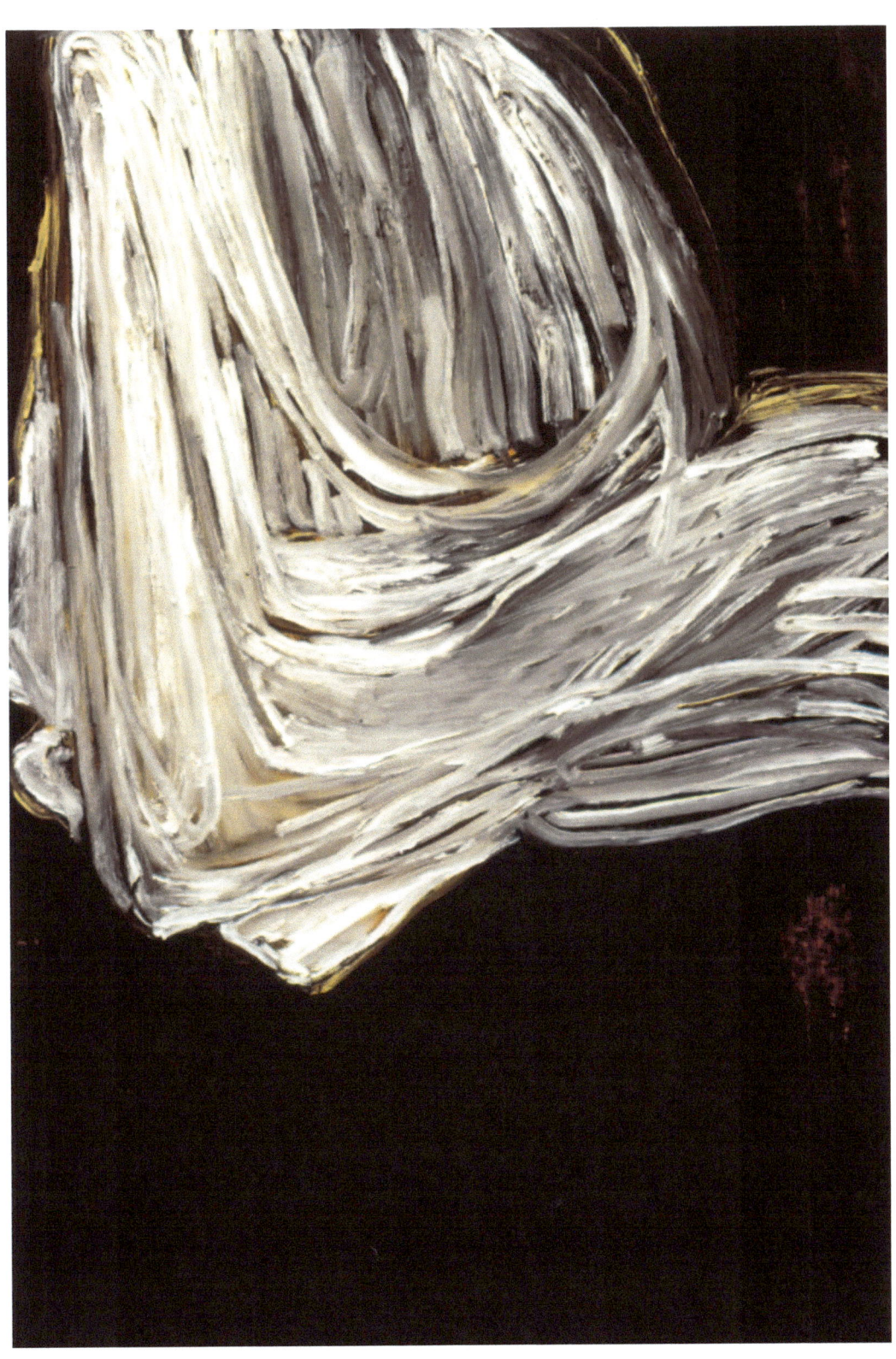

Under the Expanse   72" x 60" oil on canvas 1993

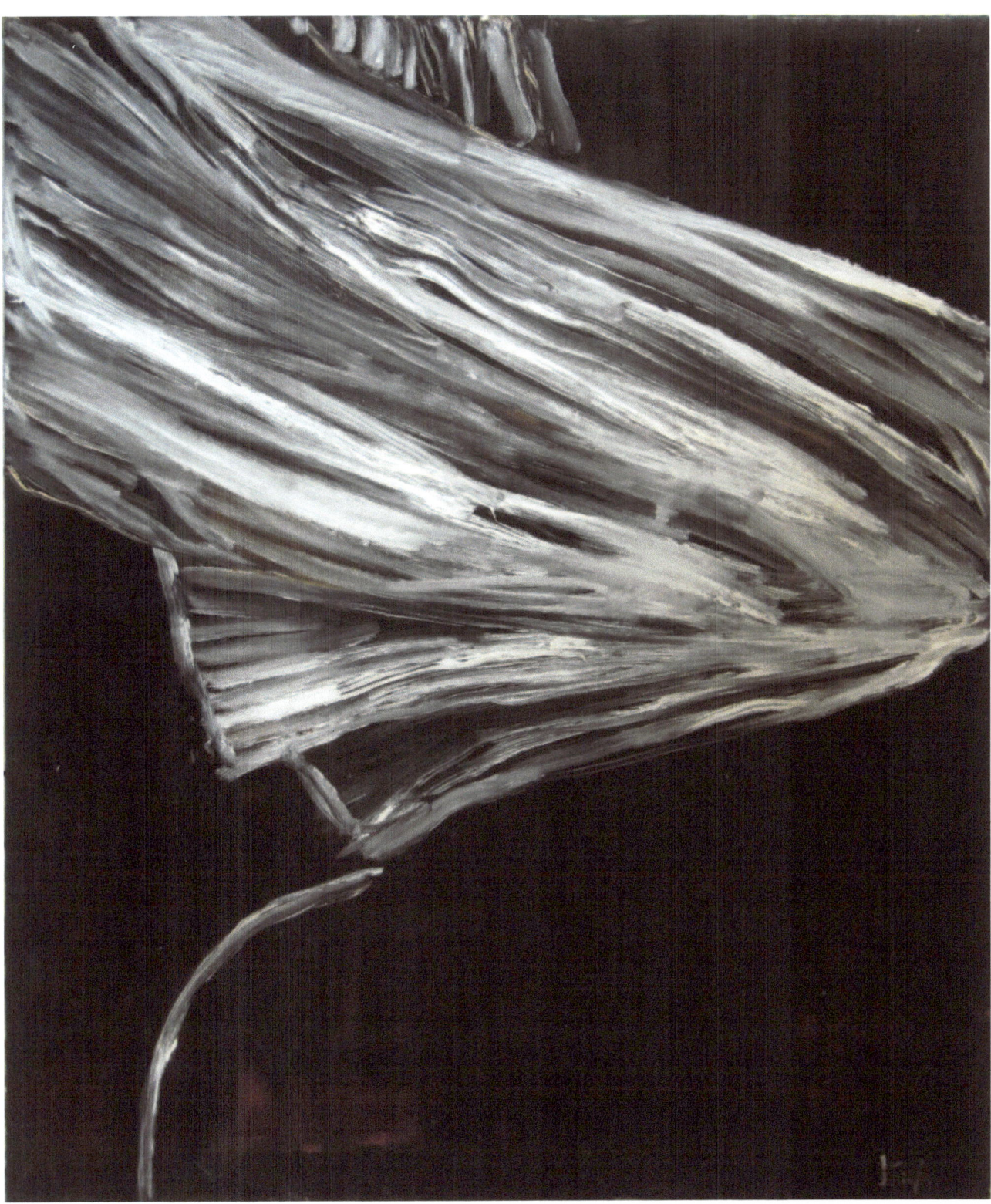

Sanctuary   72" x 48" oil on canvas 1993

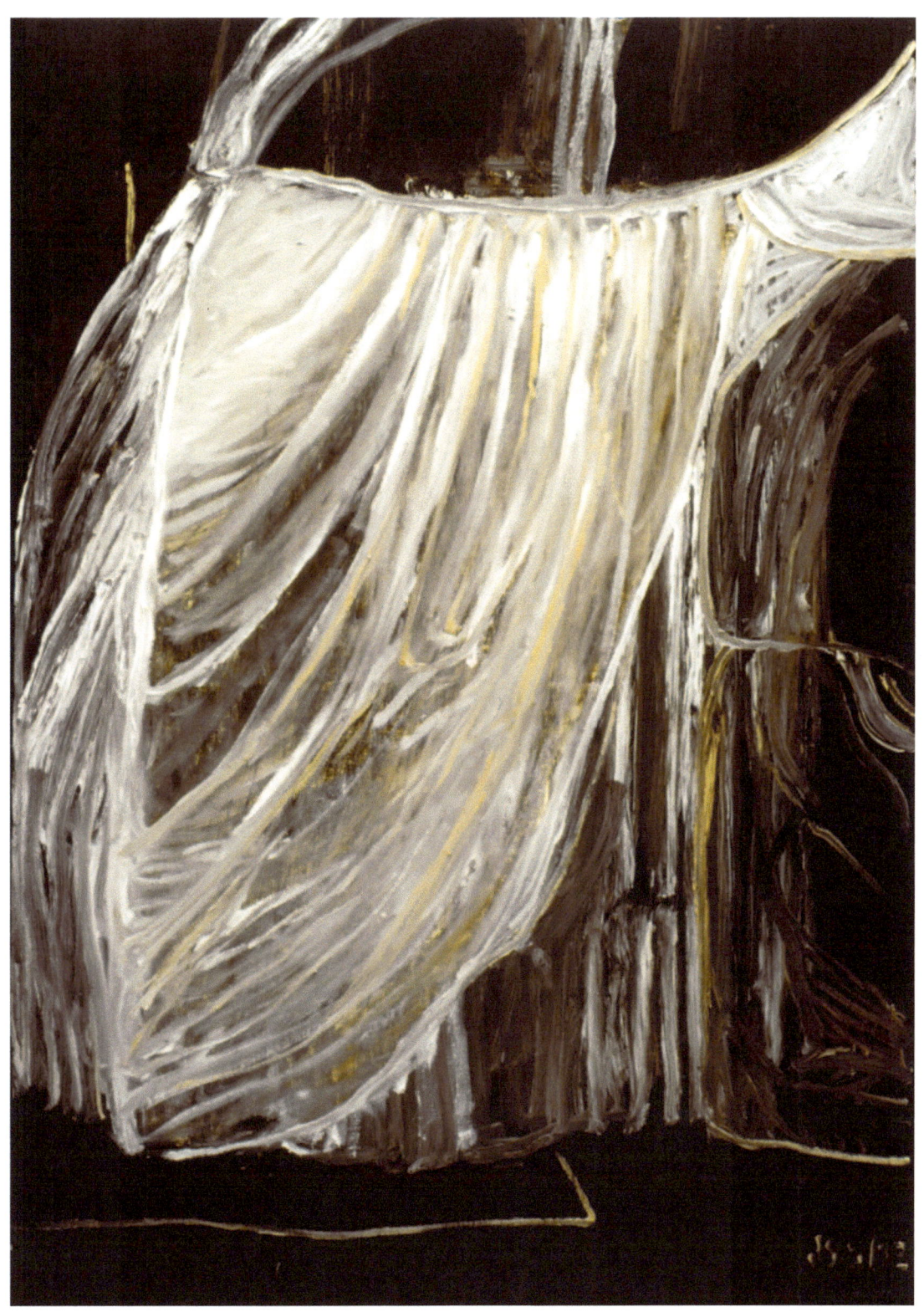

The Tempter   72″ x 60″ oil on canvas 1993

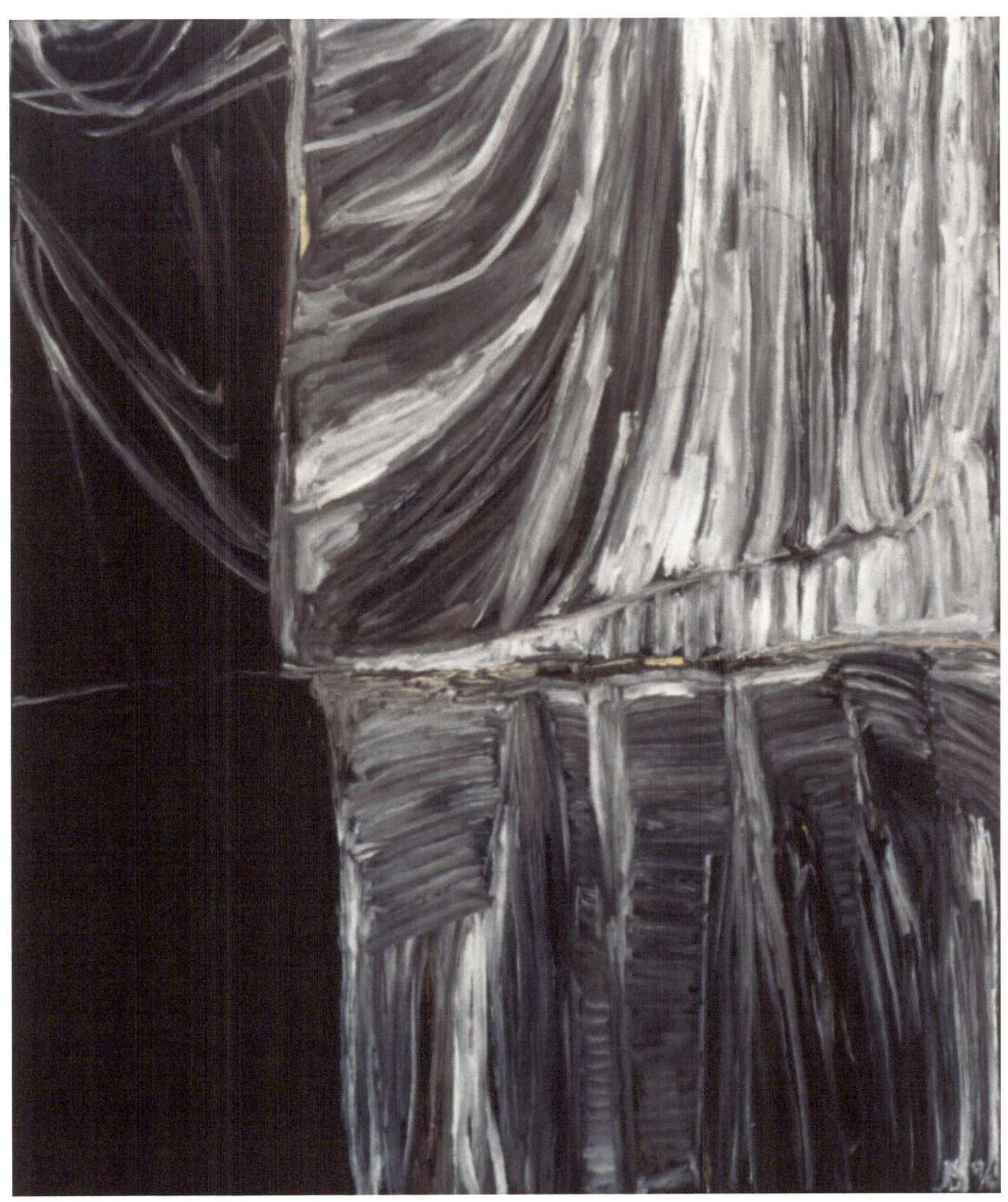

Day of Trouble 72" x 60" oil on canvas 1993

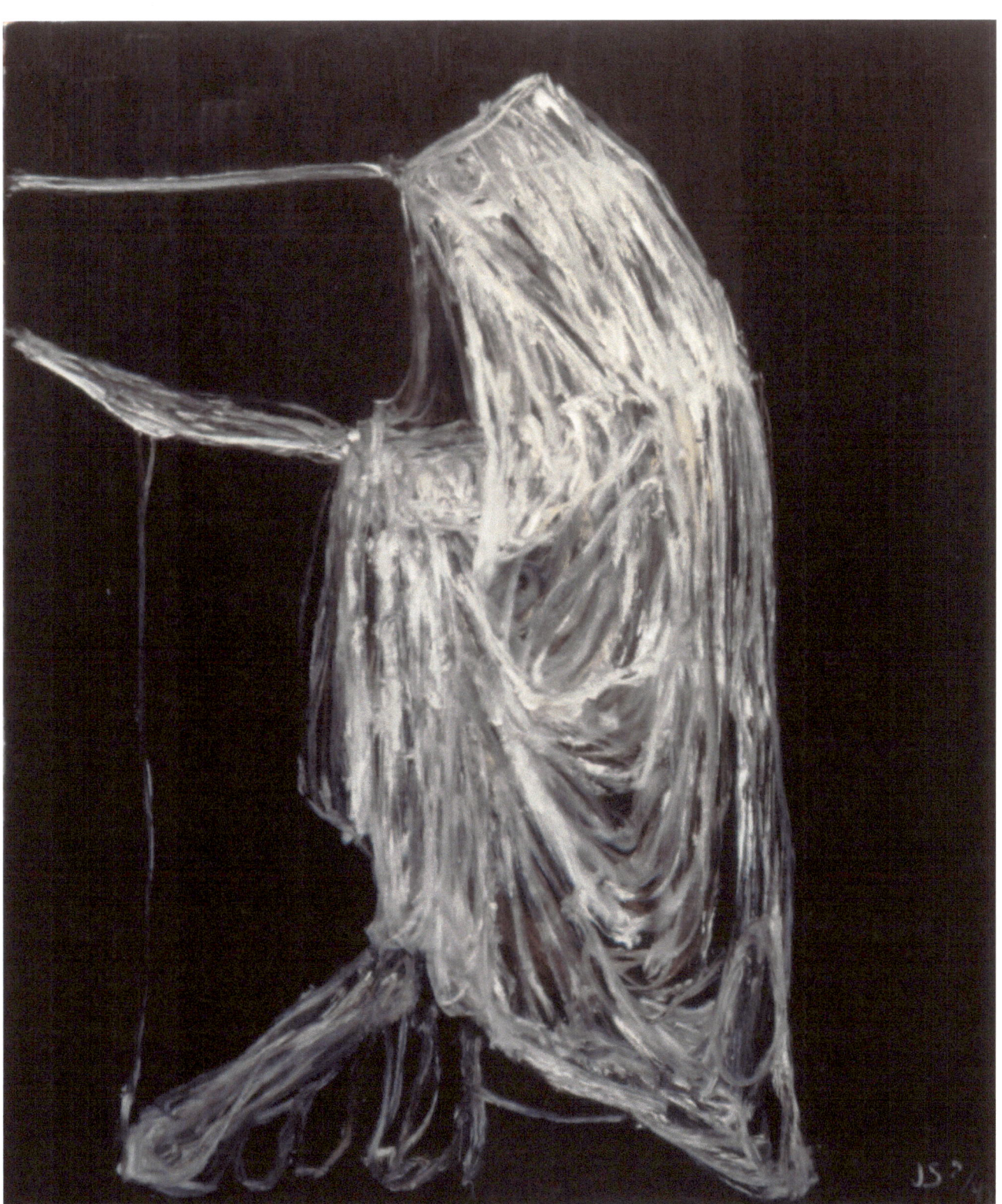

Man of Earth 72" x 48" oil on canvas 1993

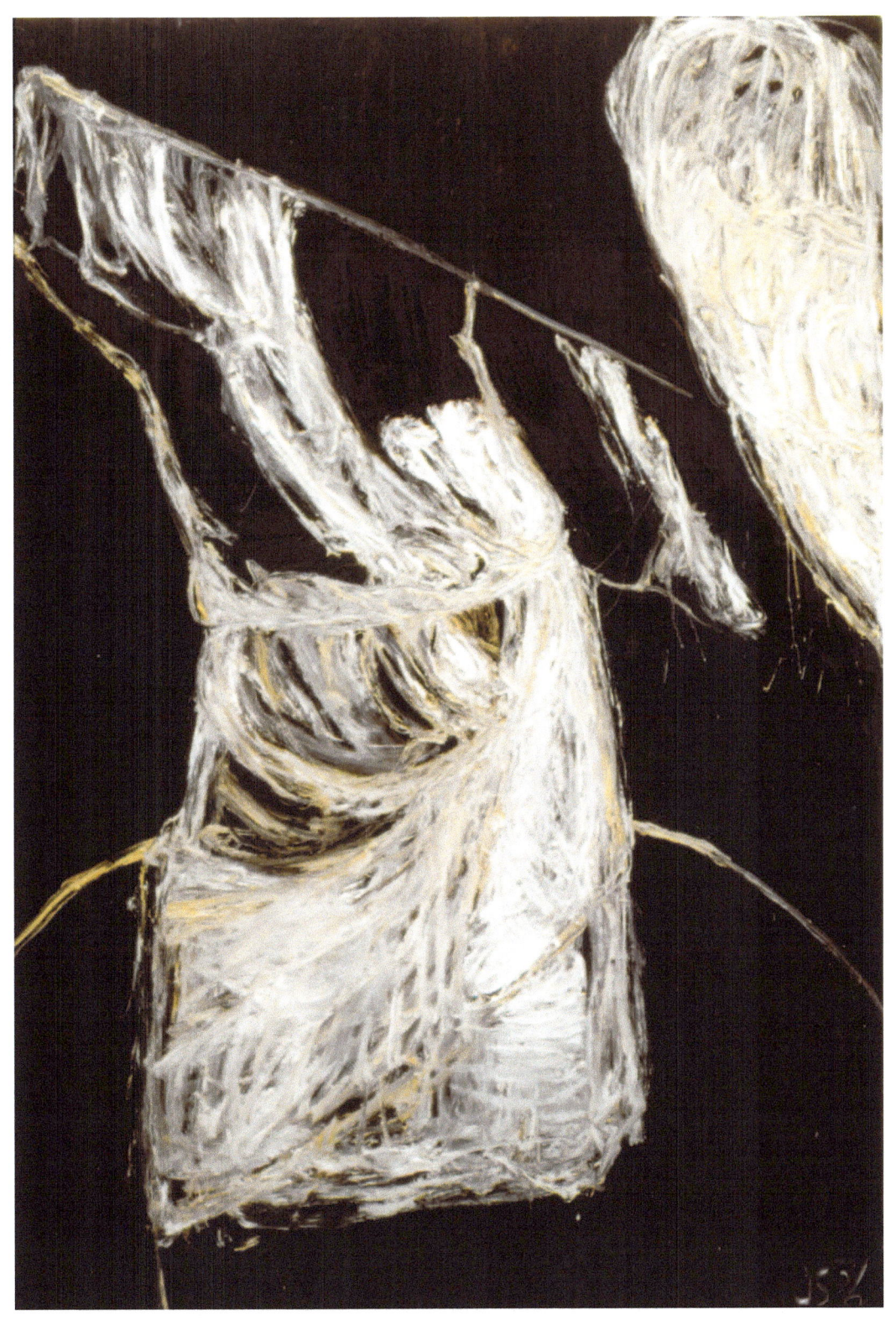

Power of the Dog 72" x 48" oil on canvas 1994

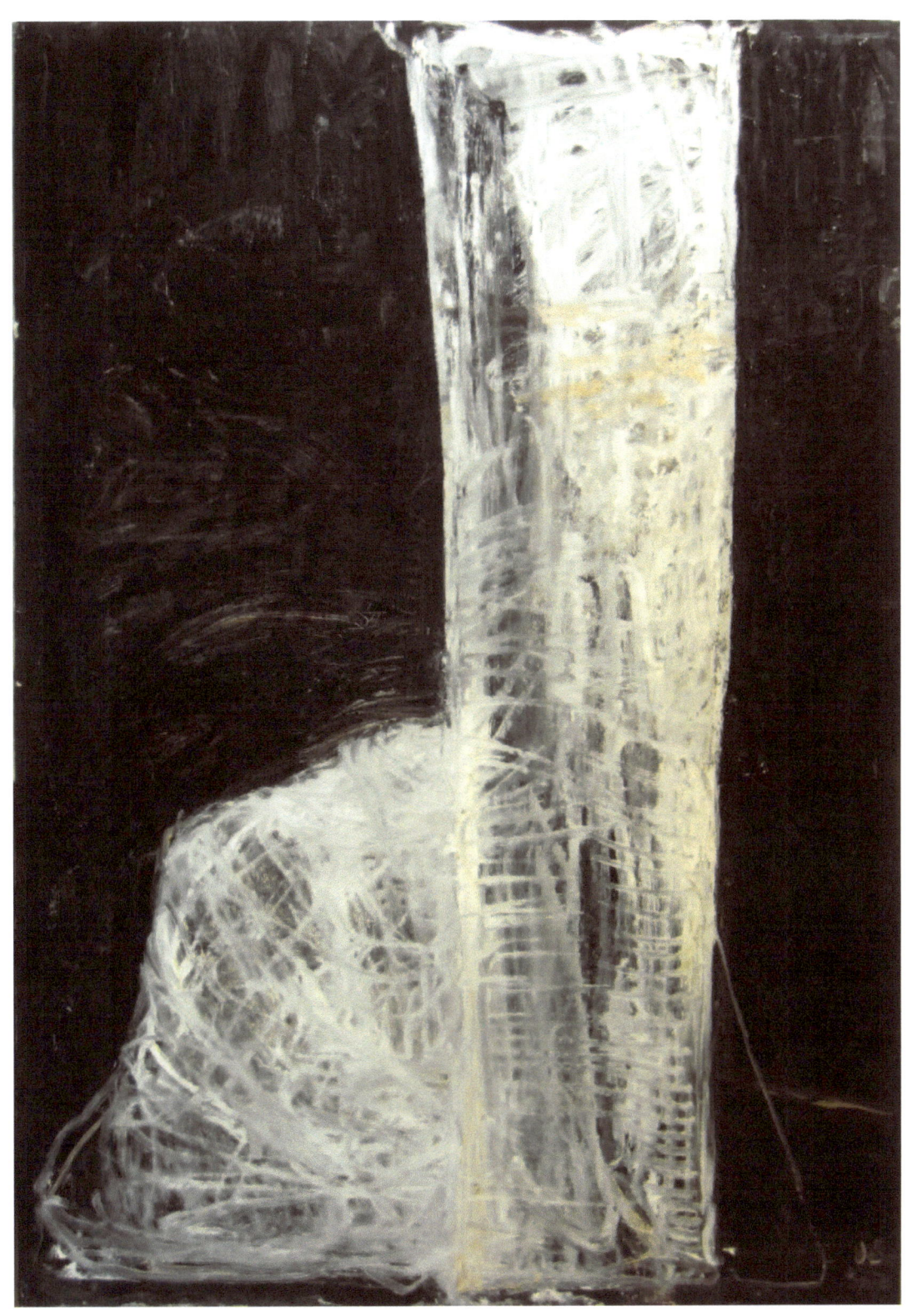

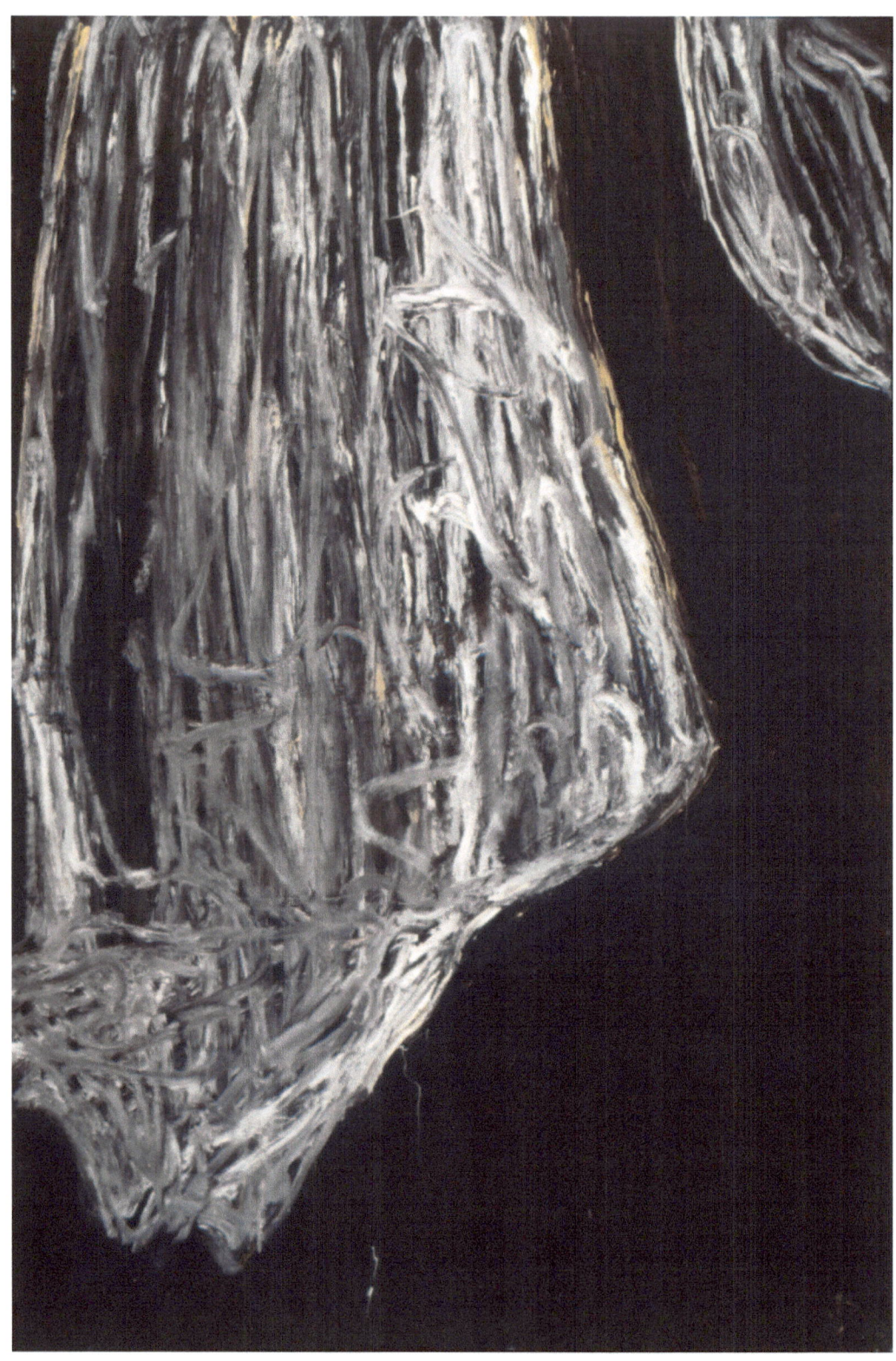

More than the Watchmen 72" x 48" oil on canvas 1993

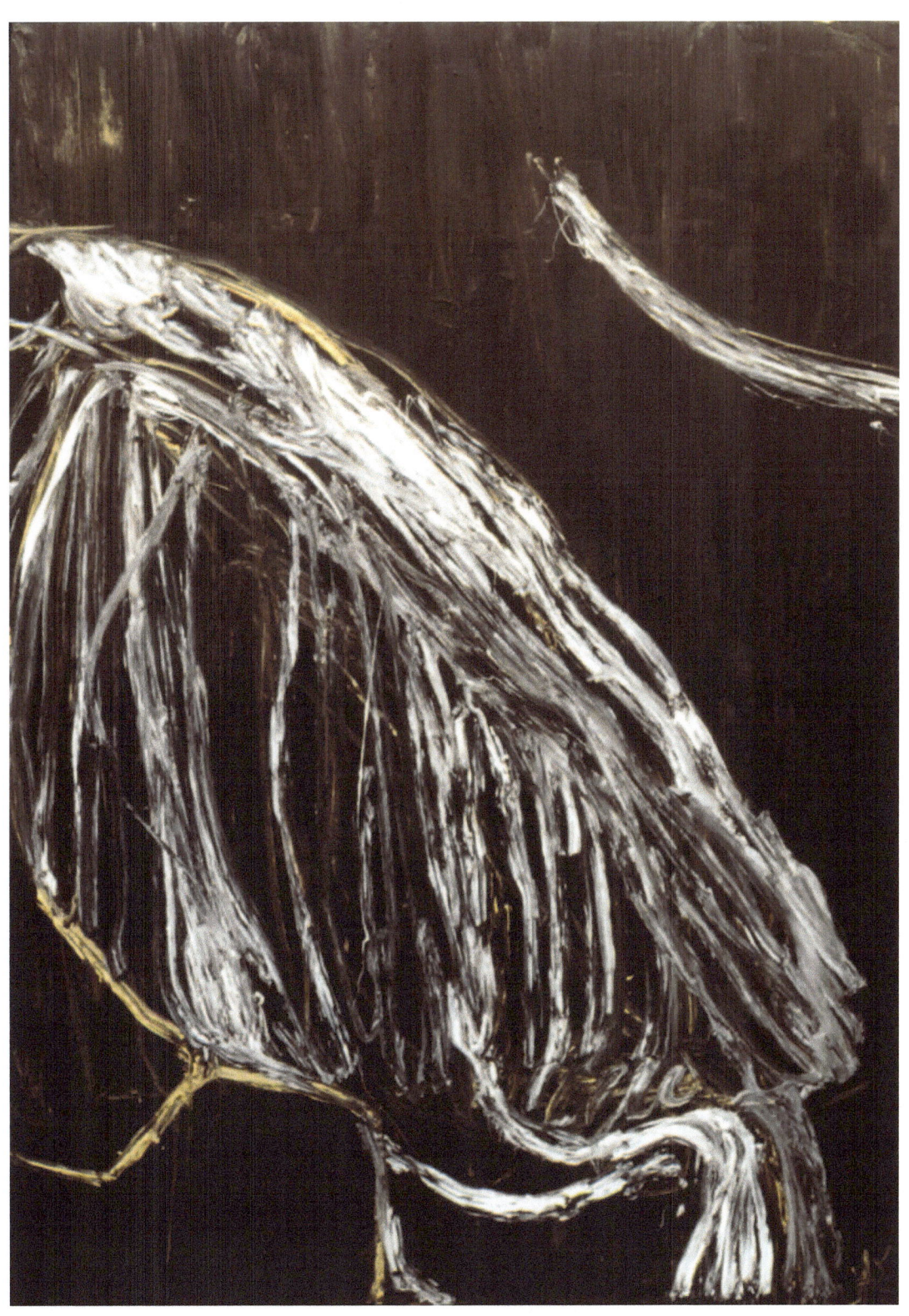

Day of Calamity 72" x 48" oil on canvas 1994

Inner Court 68" x 48" oil on canvas 1994

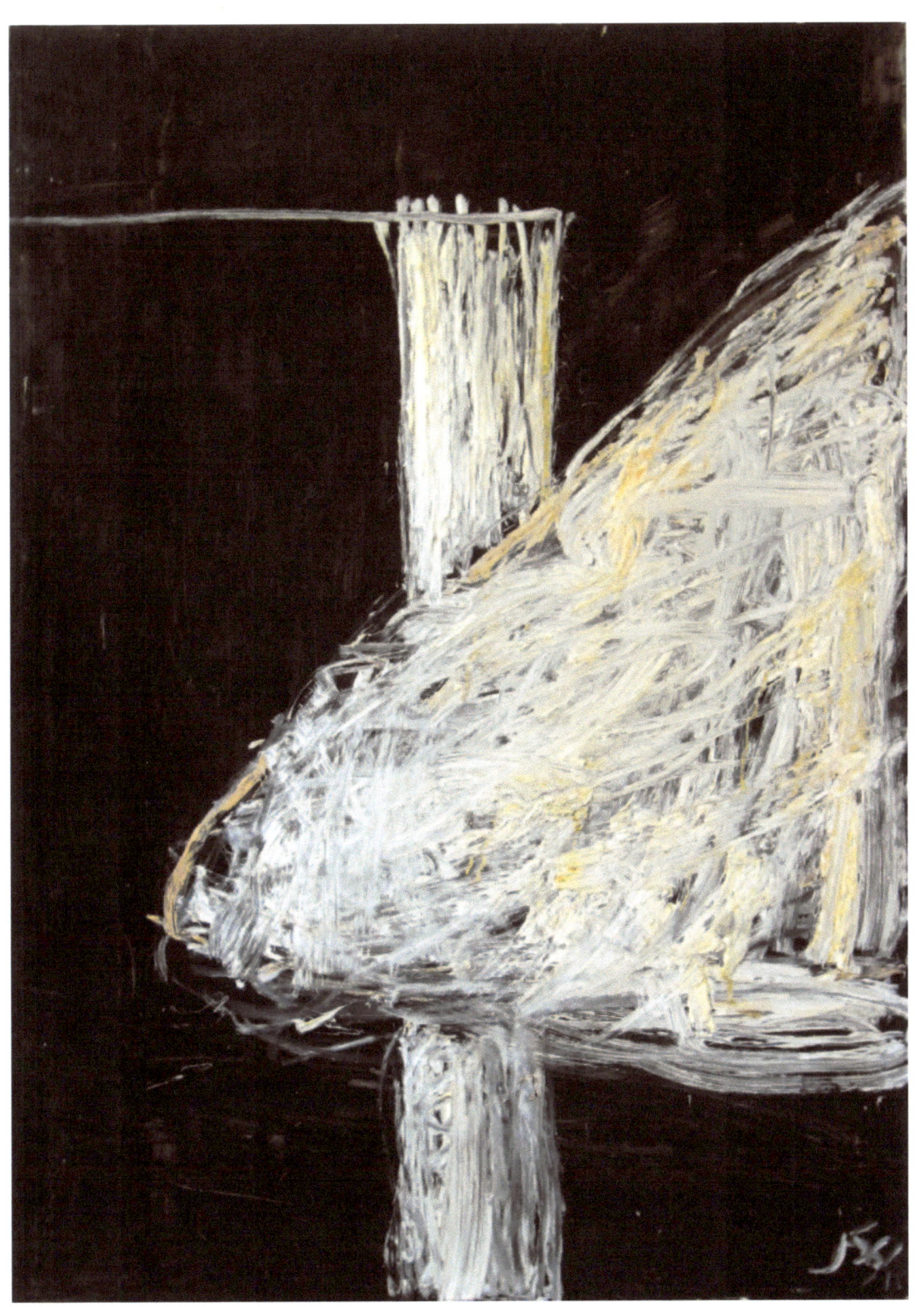

Covenant 60" x 47" oil on canvas 1994

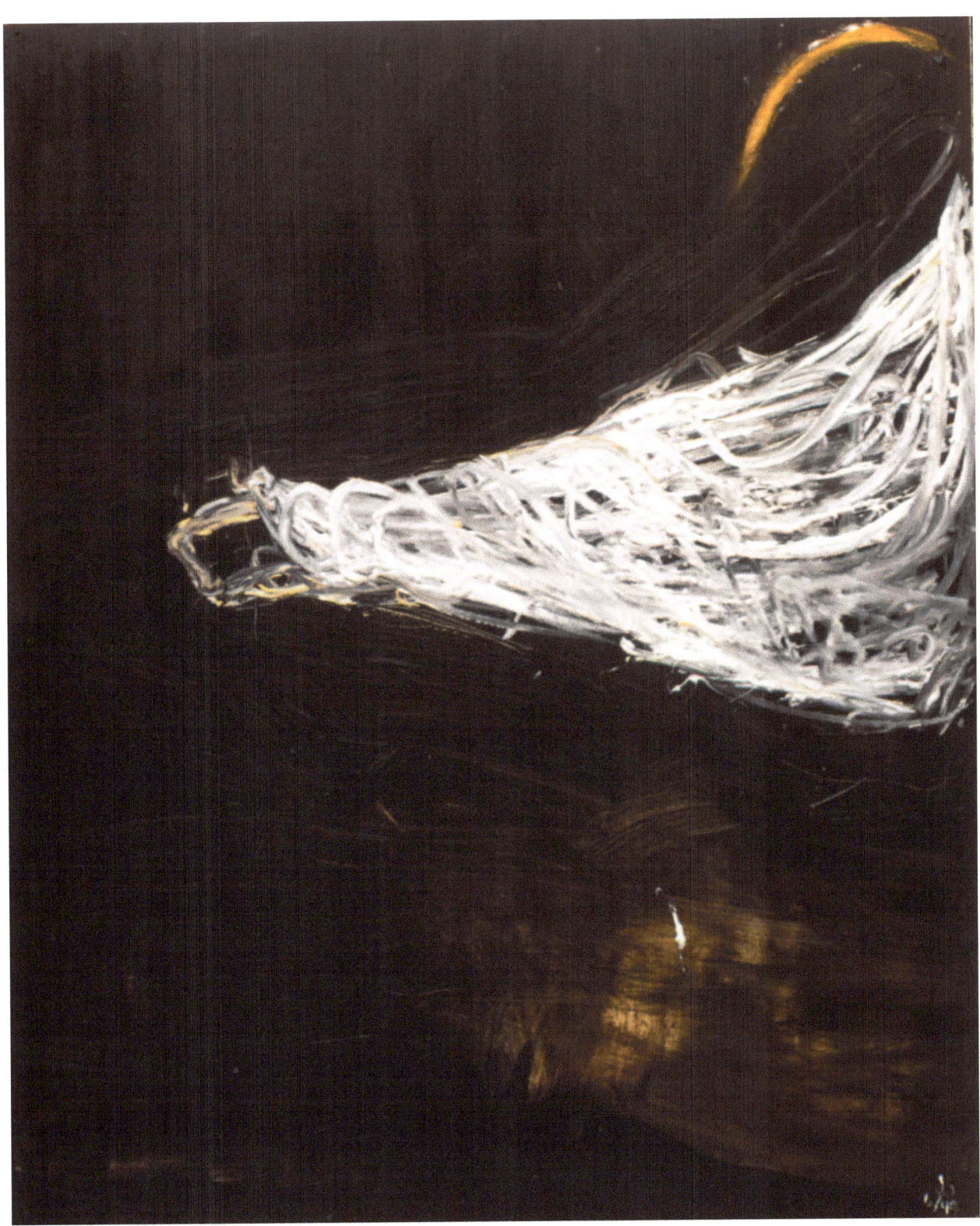

Worm   72" x 60"   oil on canvas   1994

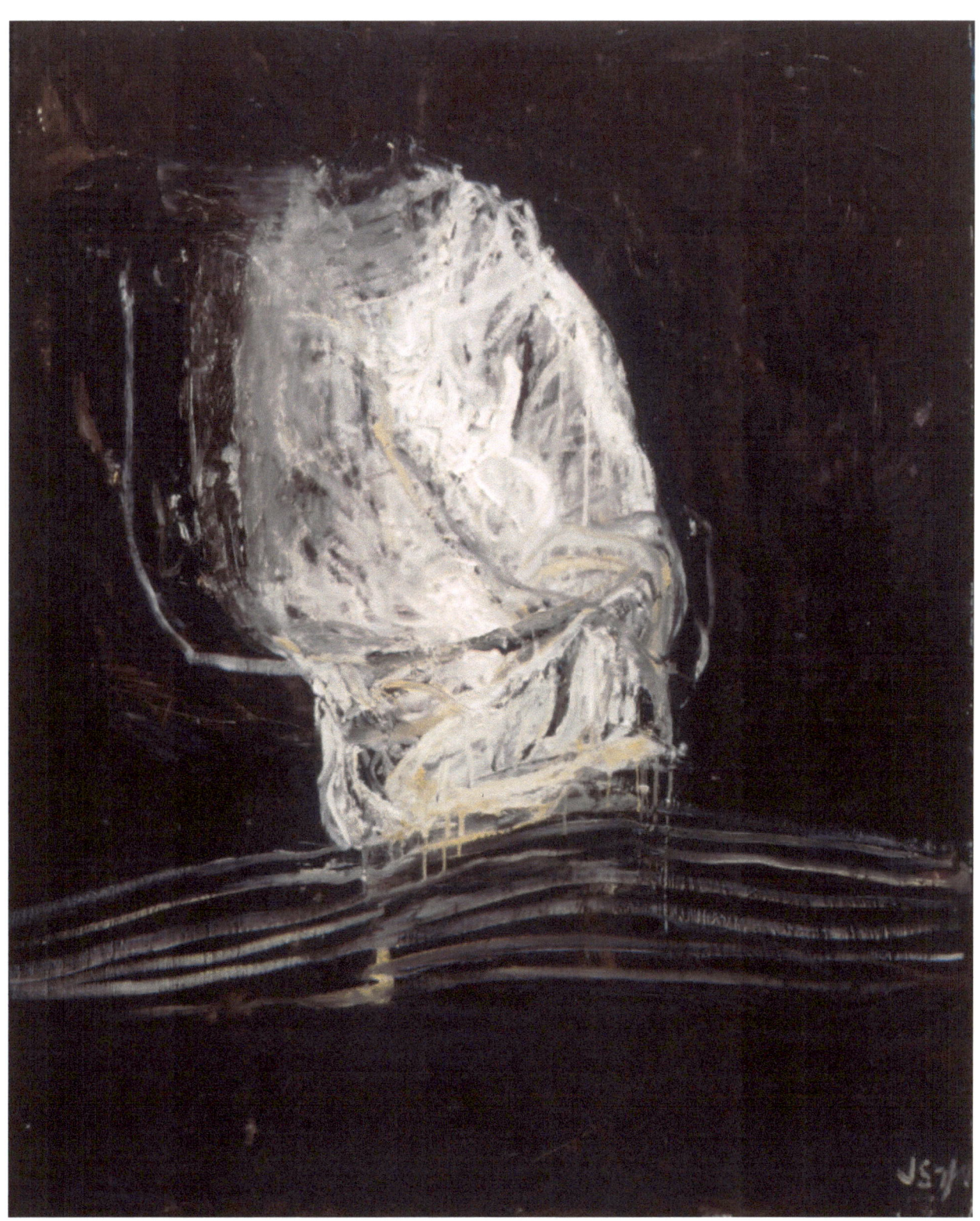

Down into Silence 72" x 60" oil on canvas   1994

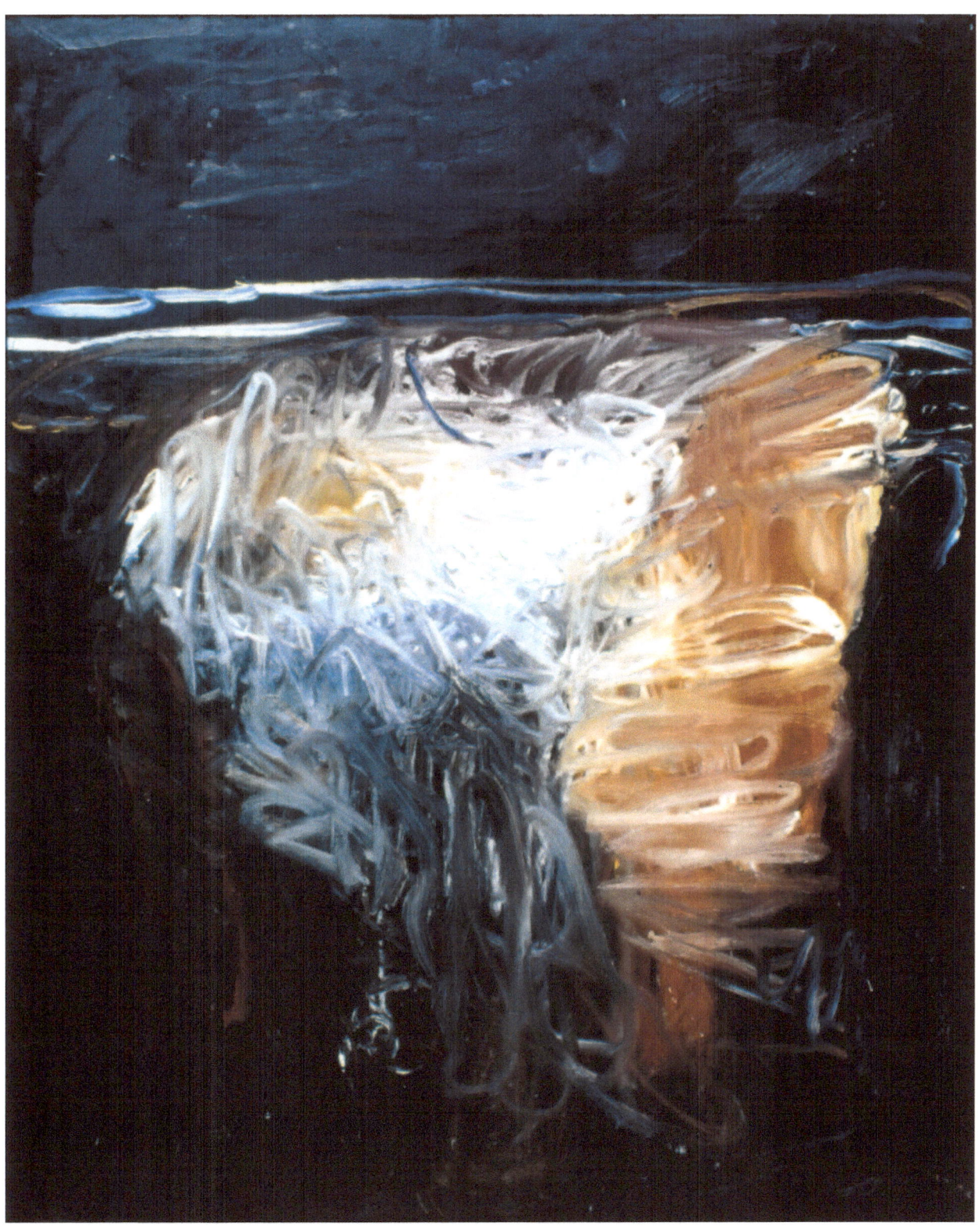

Like Water into Bones 72" x 48" oil on canvas 1994

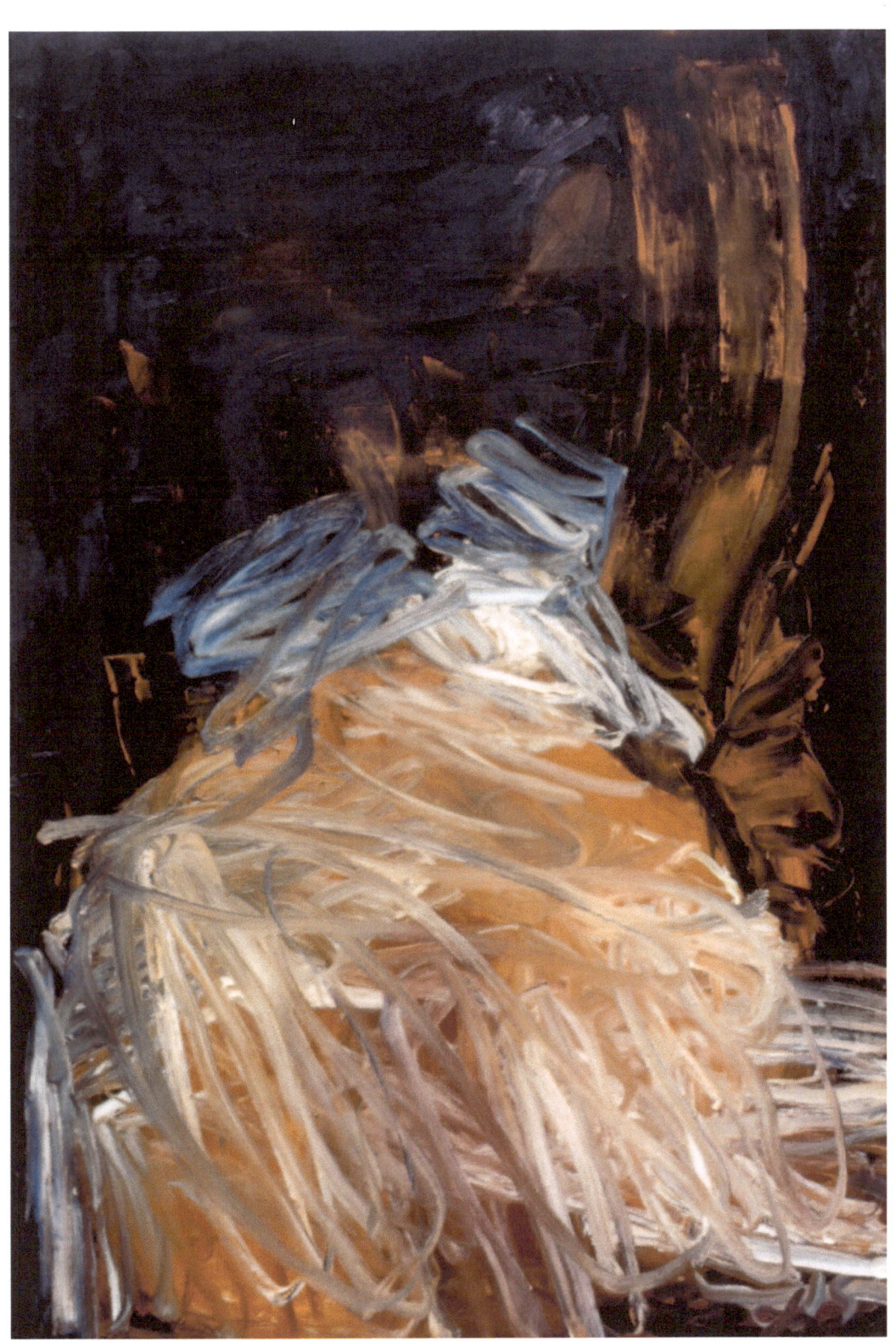

Cords of Death 60" x 48" oil on canvas   1994

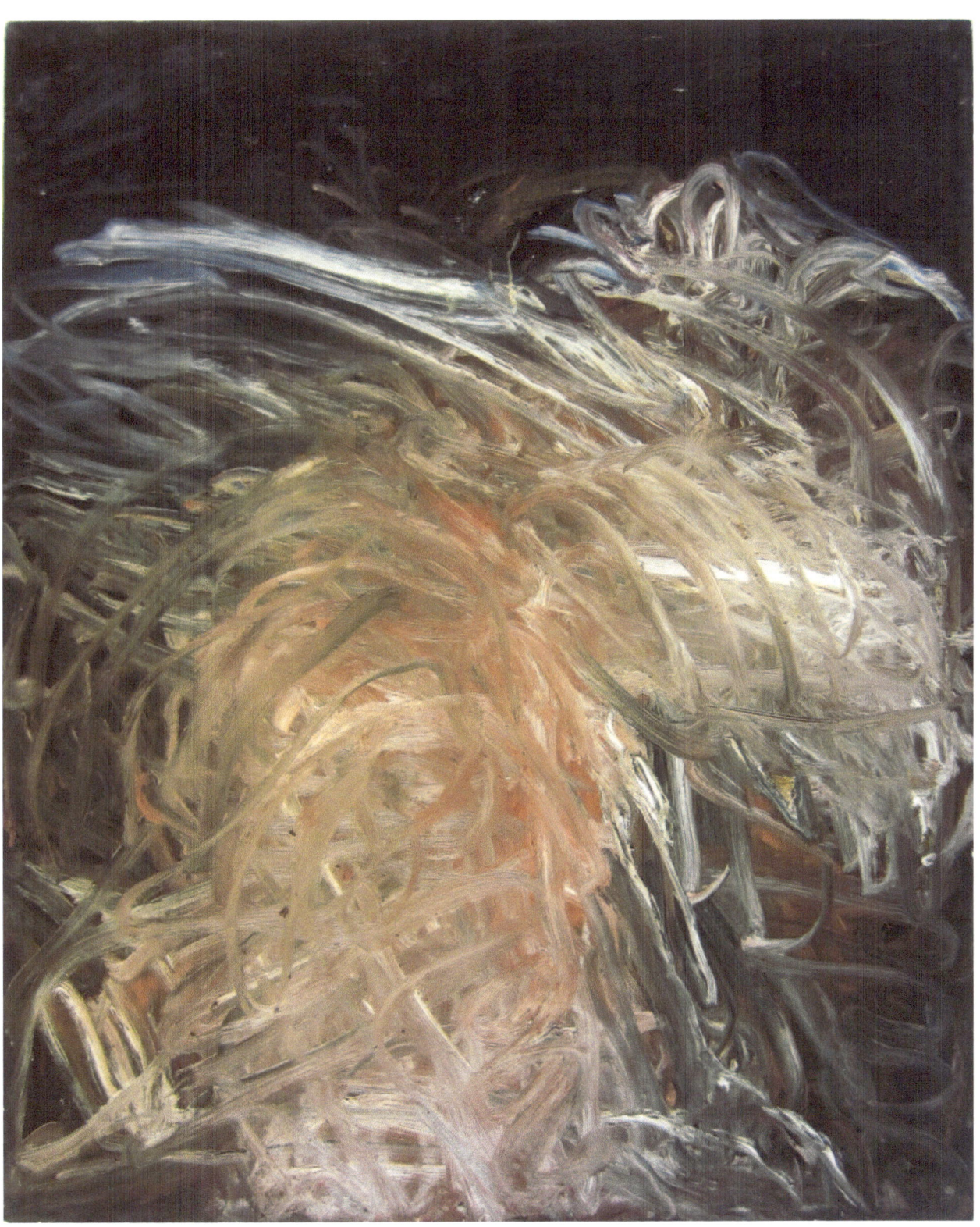

Survival Suit for a Drowning Man 68" x 48" oil on canvas   1994

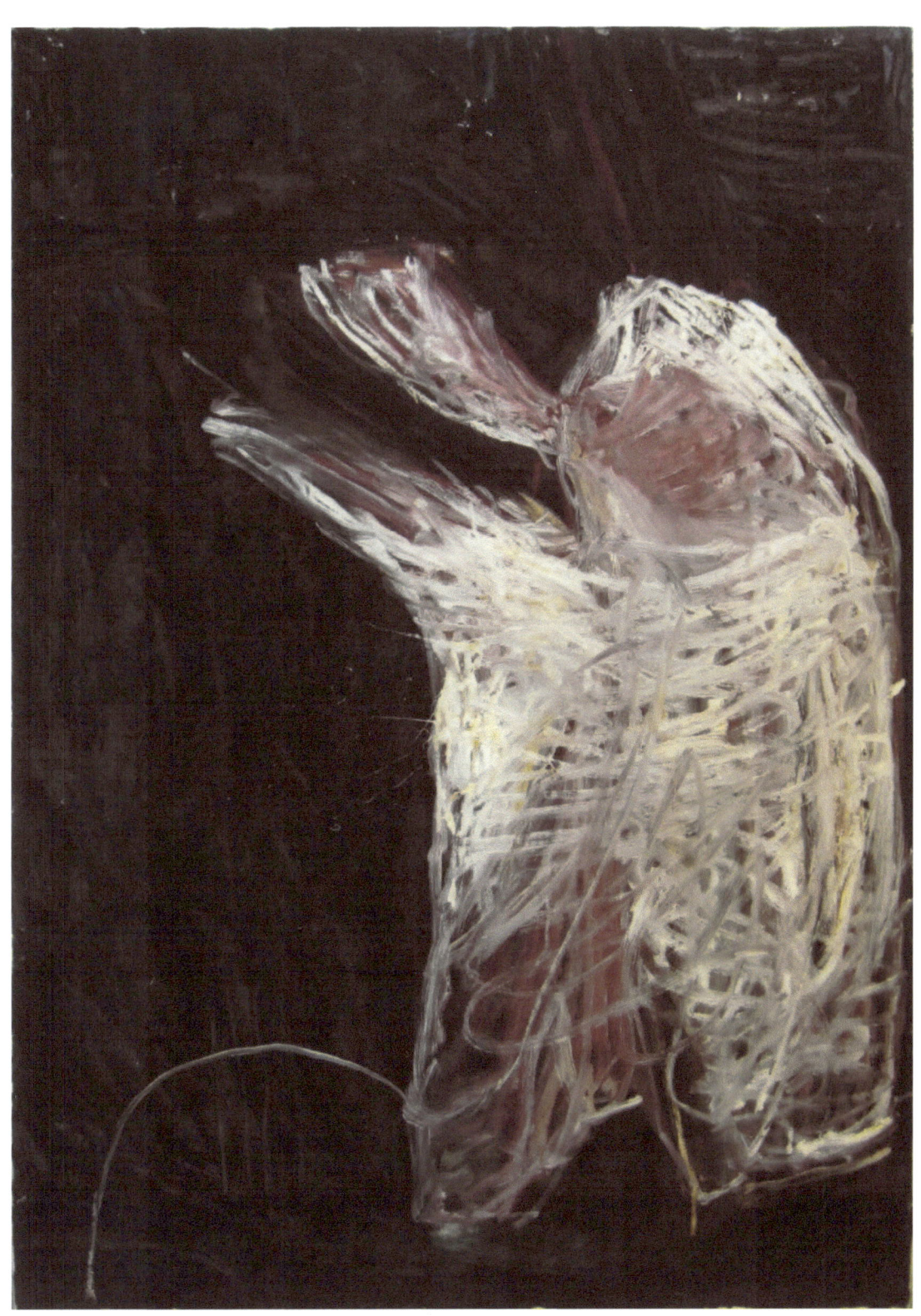

Psalms and Prophets

Jill Scipione's work is about the human condition; the situation of the soul and flesh described using the physicality of drawing and painting space. The paintings gathered under the title *Psalms and Prophets* differ from her paintings that would immediately precede or follow them not only in their direct connection to specific phrases and passages in the Biblical texts, but also in that in each, the artist uses these texts as inspiration for the building of a system or specific form in paint that would have its own meaning and object-quality. Each painting then becomes a physical model that embodies or serves as a companion to the textual concept.

The thematic purpose of the series is an existential one, asking questions about our suffering, our safety, our purpose.

"Where is safety? "

Reading through the titles of the paintings in Jill Scipione's series: *Destruction at Noonday, Terror by Night, Day of Trouble, Snare of the Fowler, Cords of Death* –on the one hand, and *I Will Deliver Him, Tent, Covenant, Messenger, Darkness is not Dark, Radiant Being* –on the other, we can see the artist's search for insight into this question. The phrases speak of threat and protection, fear and safety, destruction and deliverance. All are taken from the Biblical book of Psalms and the Prophetic books: Isaiah, Ezekiel and Hosea, amongst others. These are themes that run through the 150 collected songs and prayers of the Psalms, and the books that chronicle the efforts of the Hebrew prophets to communicate what they heard from God. The scholar Abraham Heschel called the prophets "men whose image is our refuge in distress"

"To us injustice is injurious to the welfare of the people; to the prophets it is a deathblow to existence; to us, an episode, to them, a catastrophe, a threat to the world. The situation of a person immersed in the prophet's words is one of being exposed to a ceaseless shattering of indifference." (A Heschel, *The Prophets)*

Injustice, terror, catastrophe and war were as rampant in the days these books were written as they are today. The lamentations, hopes and prayers of the psalmists and prophets enduring these real-life circumstances employ and evoke both image and symbol. It is from this viewpoint that Jill Scipione investigates and gives form to these visions, and searches for meaning.

Looking to the titles once more we can find an emphasis on nouns, (*Tent, Snare, Arrow, Wheels, Scaffolding*) that affirm the physicality of the image. In her paintng, we see the invention of a sense of object and place that is emphatic in purpose and meaning, and that makes use of the possibilities of both abstract and representational tradition to convey its subject. She is giving us a guidebook–a lectionary–so we can recognize both help and danger when they come. How do we miss the doorway that will provide our escape? By not being able to see it, or not recognizing it, if we do see. The tent will cover us, the scaffolding will allow us to ascend, we can avoid the snare, the wheels can take us away or bring us aid–but we need to know what they look like. Scipione makes use of the collected language of 20th century abstraction: gestural brushstrokes and a build-up of mark-making, light over dark; tracing schematic systems that describe a deep, unknown place–a mystery that seeks to match the soul's depths.

As the series continues, object and place turn to person/protagonist--the nouns now become active players in a drama unfolding from painting to painting. With *Messenger, Radiant Being, Servant, Magi* and *Tempter*, the paint itself changes, becomes more elegantly applied, the forms more pure. For these painting ,she begins to turn to another source, searching for a material image that embodies the sense of human hope and despair of her subject, and finding it in the volumetric figures of the early Renaissance painter, Giotto. The humanity and genuineness of Giotto's people, caught up in their encounter with Christ and their struggle with faith, becomes the second text for this series. Perhaps one can see Giotto as continuing the work of the Biblical writers, describing and creating a reality that he could not have seen but somehow perceives through the people around him and the process of making his art.

The ravaged scrawled density of *Snare* or *Darkness is not Dark* gives way to the smoothly layered *Messenger*, then takes another turn as the titles begin to describe situation and place. *More than the Watchmen, Power of the Dog, Covenant*, and others that follow become complex, chalkboard-light structures over deep browns and blue-blacks, threaded through with glimpses of a golden line that increases as the set of work finally goes down in flames of color. As we see Scipione progressing through the series, it becomes clear that she does not allow the abstract elements alone to dictate the direction that the series takes. She invents and reinvents for each concept, staying with each mode for only as many paintings as it takes to realize the idea. Somewhat like the prophets themselves, she is led by her need to communicate the message.

The last few paintings return to the beginning. With *Worm* and *Down into Silence*, the promise declared in *I Will Deliver Him* at the start of the series seems to be lost. The series dies beautifully, if not peacefully, thrashing about as if the figure, now real and no longer ideal, is trying to emerge from the bonds of the paint itself–free itself from the light or emerge into the light? The outcome is unclear, uncertain whether the drowning man of the final paintings will be saved–or will the waters rebirth him? The final image, *Survival Suit for a Drowning Man*, is an outline of Giotto's John the Baptis– just the robe, the body only as a dark space, an arm reaching out. Around this time, the artist was visiting maritime museums to look at the full-body, red, survival suits that would keep sailors alive in the cold waters of the Great Lakes. With this additional contemporay influence, the Giotto image in this painting becomes a different form, almost unrelated to the source. This device is similar to methods often employed by artist Jasper Johns in his works, which come from a Pop Art or Conceptual Art perspective, and point to a direction that Scipione's work would take in the future, as she turned more and more to the manipulation and transformation of the object.

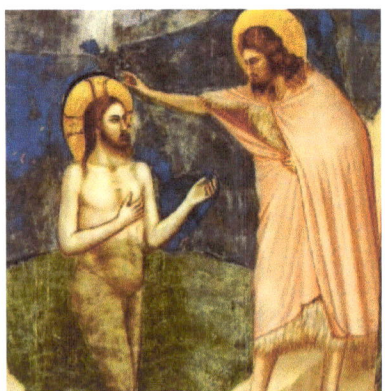

Fig. 1 Giotto, The Baptism of Christ

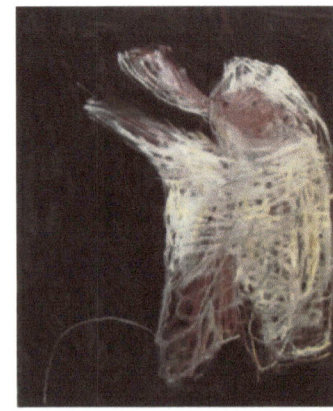

Fig. 2 Survival Suit for a Drowning Man, detail

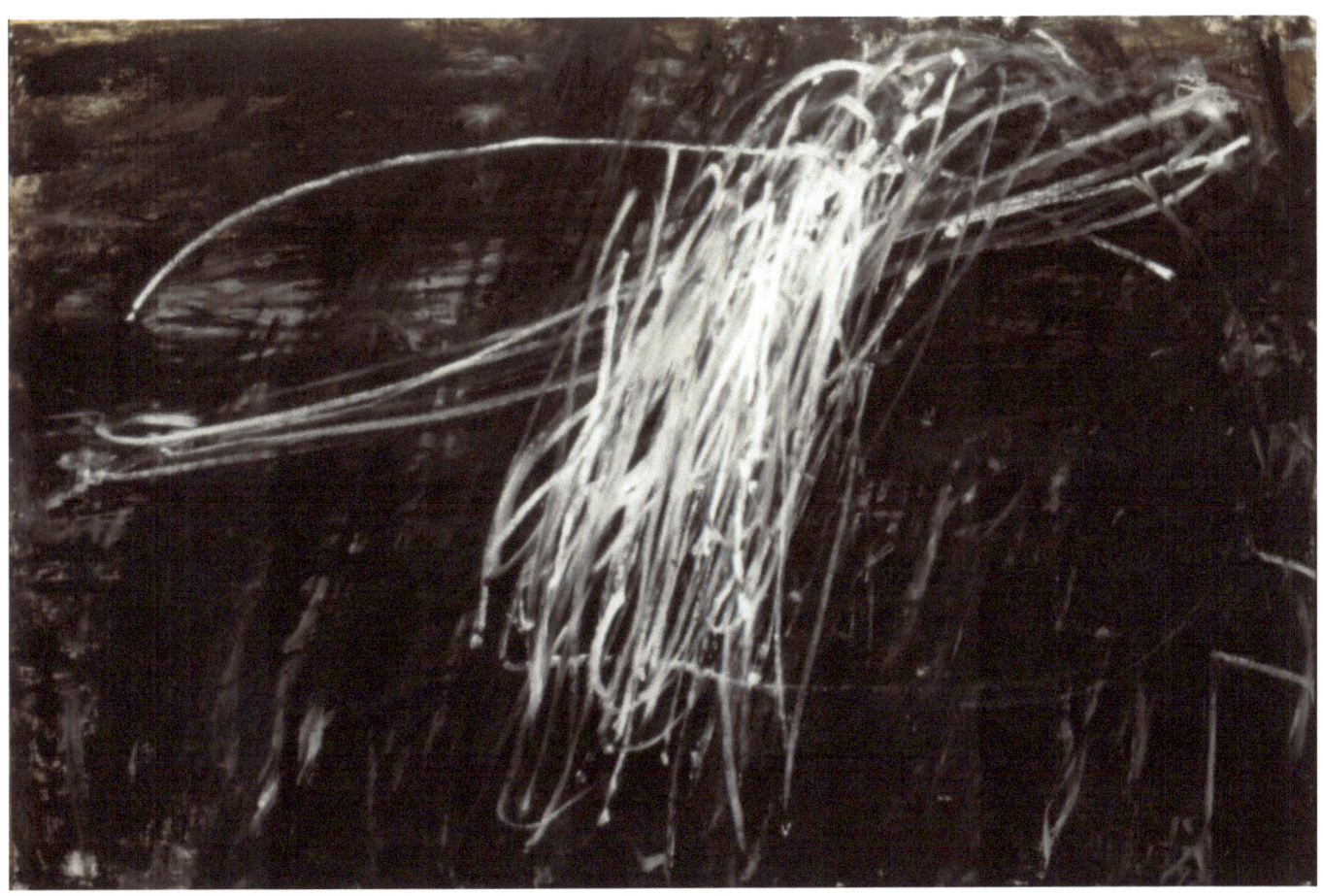

Arrow of Daytime 72" x 108" oil on linen 1992

In the series of drawings and paintings that follow, Scipione would revisit Giotto's works, recording, deconstructing re-ordering and reforming them into new objects–and then apply similar methods to cuts of meat, and later, human skulls and bones; creating systems of objects that, as they become ever more clearly realized and identified, suggest greater depths of meaning. These images, imbued with a sense of reality–of what the artist refers to as an 'actual-ness'–continue to offer an answer, order and purpose–her search for a way in which things will be made clearer and more visible.

James Pustorino

Director, Drawing Rooms

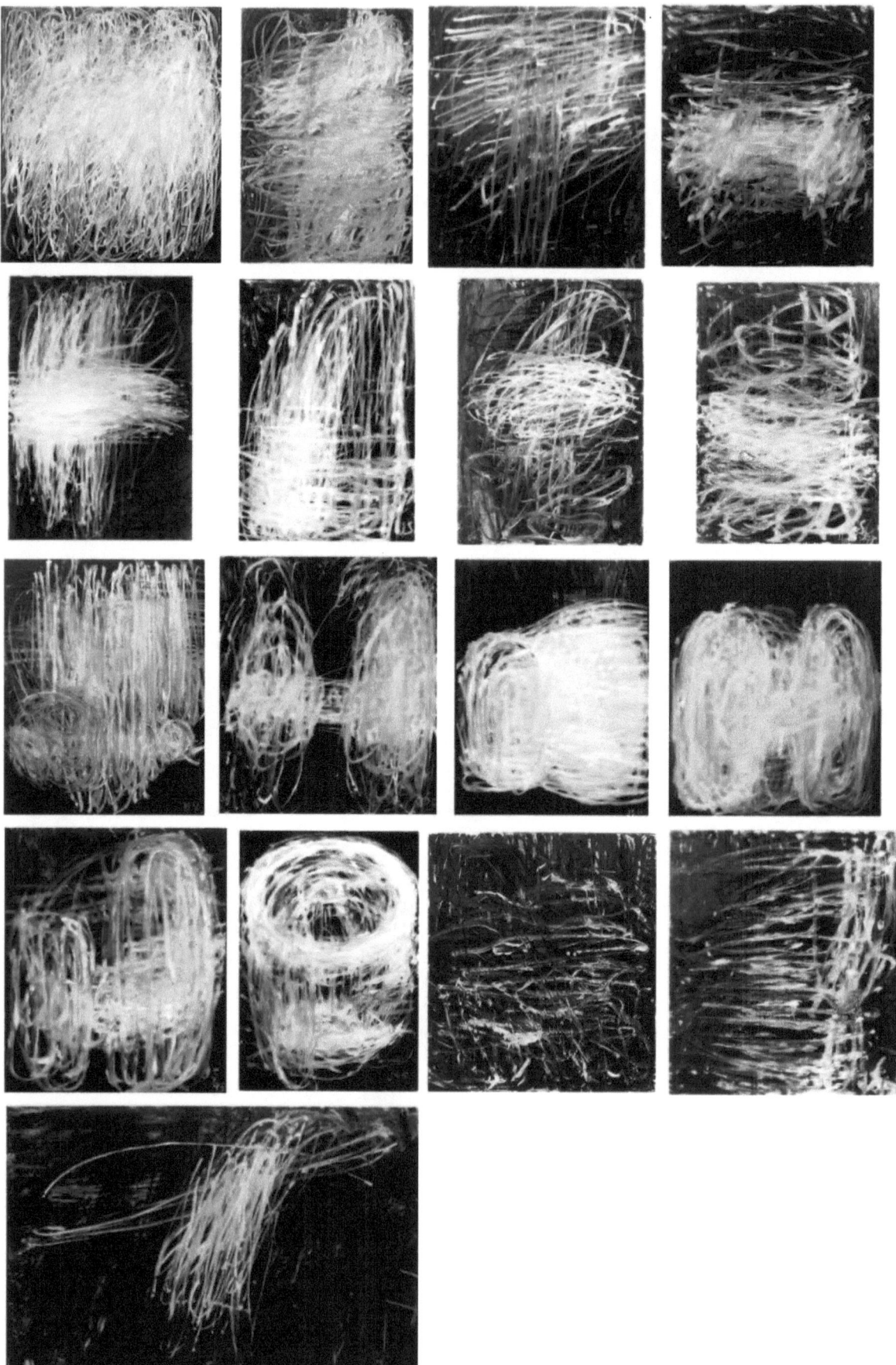

Catalogue of Works with Biblical References

Destruction at Noonday 72" x 60" oil on canvas 1992
Psalm 91:6

I Will Deliver Him 72" x 46" oil on canvas 1992
Psalm 91:14,15 Because he clings to me I will deliver him; because he knows my name I will set him on high. 15 He will call upon me and I will answer; I will be with him in distress; I will deliver him and give him honor.

Terror by Night 60" x 48" oil on linen 1992
Psalm 91:5

Expanse 60" x 48" oil on canvas 1993
Ezekiel 1:22 Ez 10:1

Tent 72" x 48" oil on linen 1992
Psalm 27:5

Height 72" x 48" oil on canvas 1993
Romans 8:39

Snare of the Fowler 72" x 48" oil on linen 1992
Psalm 91:3 He will rescue you from the fowler's snare, and from the destroying plague,

Scaffolding 72" x 48" oil on linen 1993

Conveyance 60" x 48" oil on linen 1993

Chariot 72" x 60" oil on canvas 1993
2Kings 2:11,12 & 13:14 Ps 68: 104:3 Is 66:15 Ez 26:7, 10 Joel 2:5 Rev 9:9

In the Midst of the Wheels 67" x 48" oil on canvas 1993
Ezekiel 10: 10-13

Wheels 72" x 60" oil on canvas 1993
Wheel in the Sky, Wheel on the Earth 72" x 48" oil on canvas 1993
Vehicle 72" x 60"   oil on canvas 1993
Ezekiel 1: 16-21   The wheels and their construction sparkled like yellow topaz, and all four of them looked the same: their construction seemed as though one wheel was inside the other. 17When they moved, they went in any of the four directions without veering as they moved. 18 The four of them had rims, high and fearsome—eyes filled the four rims all around. 19When the living creatures moved, the wheels moved with them; and when the living creatures were raised from the ground, the wheels also were raised. 20Wherever the spirit would go, they went. And they were raised up together with the living creatures, for the spirit of the living creatures was in the wheels. 21Wherever the living creatures moved, the wheels moved; when they stood still, the wheels stood still. When they were lifted up from the earth, the wheels were lifted up with them. For the spirit of the living creatures was in the wheels.

Darkness is not Dark 72" x 60" oil on canvas 1993
Psalm 139:12

Threshing Instrument with Teeth 72" x 60" oil on canvas 1993
Isaiah 41:15 "See, I will make you into a threshing sledge, new and sharp, with many teeth.You will thresh the mountains and crush them, and reduce the hills to chaff.

Arrow of Daytime 72" x 108" oil on linen   1992
Psalm 91:5

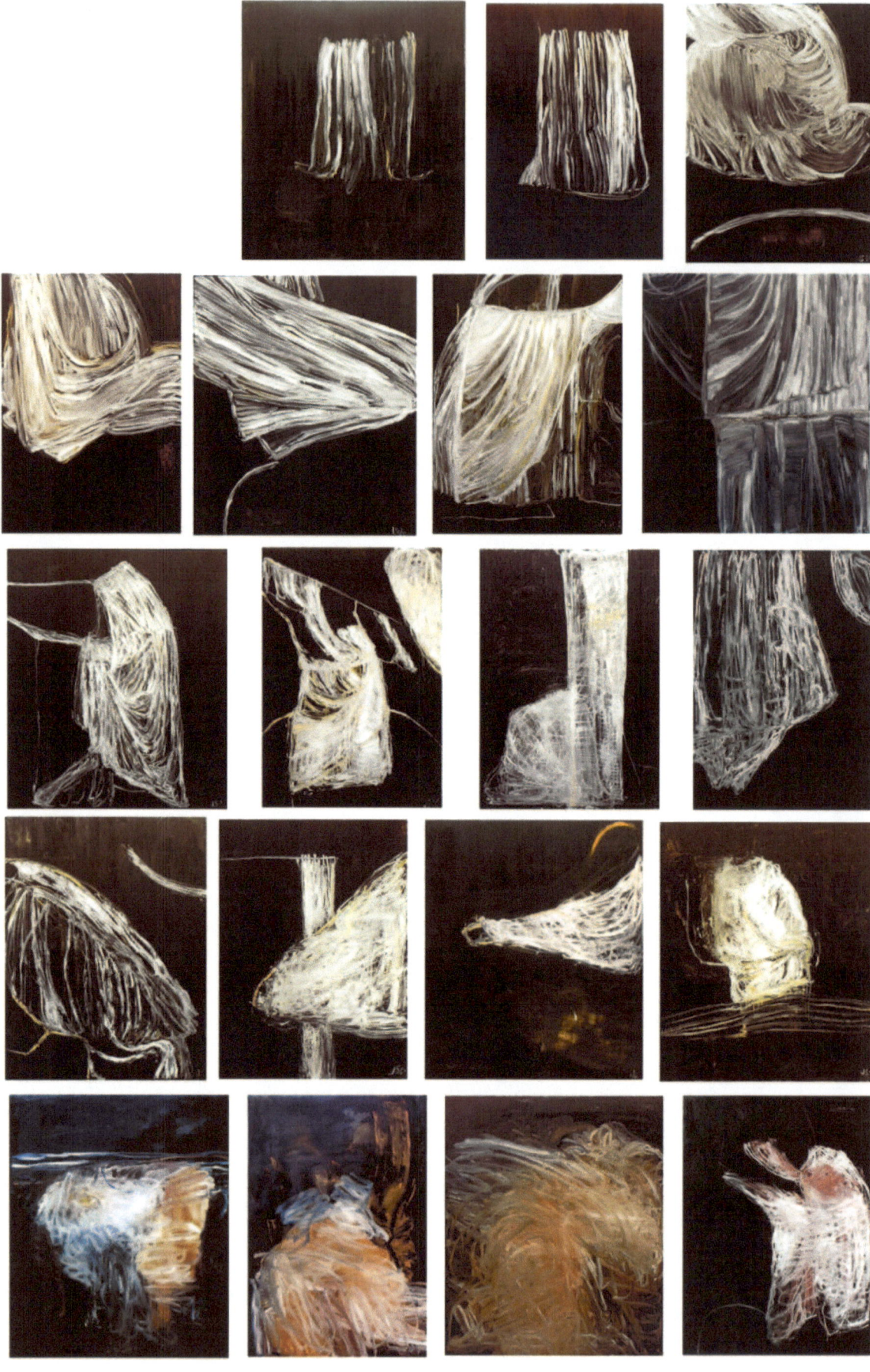

Messenger 72" x 60" oil on canvas 1993
Isaiah 41:27 42:19

Radiant Being 72" x 48" oil on canvas 1993
Psalm 34:5

Servant 72" x 48" oil on canvas   1993
Isaiah 49:5-7

Magi   72" x 48" oil on canvas 1993

Under the Expanse   72" x 60" oil on canvas 1993
Ezekiel 1:23

Sanctuary   72" x 48" oil on canvas 1993
Is 8:14 Jer 17:12 Ez 37:28

The Tempter   72" x 60" oil on canvas 1993
Matthew 4:3

Day of Trouble 72" x 60" oil on canvas 1993
Psalm 50:15   Ps 27:5

Man of Earth 72" x 48" oil on canvas 1993
1 Corinthians 15:47

Power of the Dog 72" x 48" oil on canvas 1994
Psalm 22:21 Deliver my soul from the sword, my life from the power of the dog.

More than the Watchmen 72" x 48" oil on canvas 1993
Psalm 130:6 My soul looks for the Lord more than watchmen for daybreak.
More than watchmen for daybreak,

Day of Calamity 72" x 48" oil on canvas 1994
Psalm 18:18 Obadiah1:13

Inner Court 68" x 48" oil on canvas   1994
Ezekiel 44:17, 27

Covenant 60" x 47" oil on canvas   1994
Genesis 15:9-11

Worm 72" x 60" oil on canvas   1994
Psalm 22:7

Down into Silence 72" x 60" oil on canvas 1994
Psalm 115:17 The dead do not praise the LORD, not all those go down into silence

Like Water into Bones 72" x 48" oil on canvas 1994
Psalm 109:18

Cords of Death 60" x 48" oil on canvas   1994
Psalm 116:3 18:5 The cords of death encompassed me; the torrents of destruction terrified me.
6 The cords of Sheol encircled me; the snares of death lay in wait for me.

Survival Suit for a Drowning Man 68" x 48" oil on canvas 1994

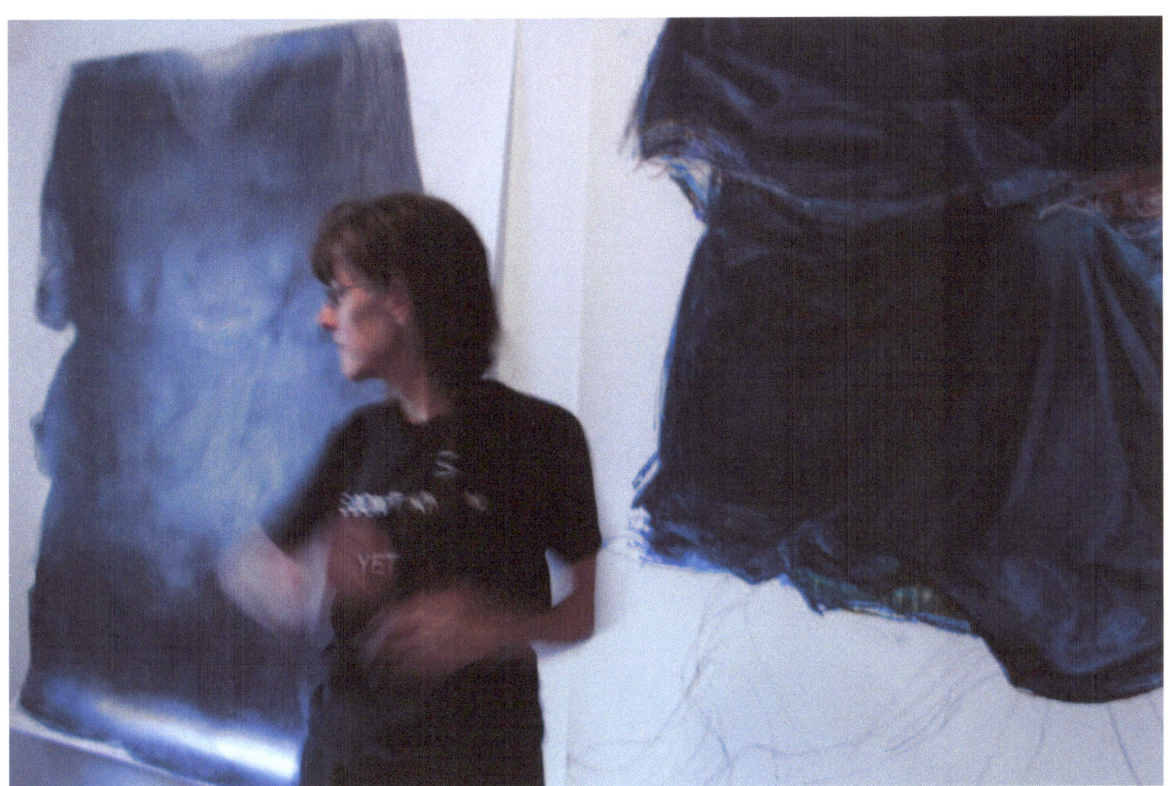

Jill Scipione was born in Ashtabula, Ohio, on Lake Erie. She received early art training at the Butler Institute of American Art when her family moved to the Youngstown area, and majored in painting at Carnegie-Mellon University where she earned her BFA. She lived in Boston, the New York City area, and Pittsburgh before returning to Ohio in the early 1990s. She started working on the Psalms and Prophets series there in a studio-shed with funds awarded through a Pollock-Krasner grant. Her work has been seen in galleries, museums, and art-spaces in New York City, New Jersey, Boston, Santa Fe, and throughout Pennsylvania and Ohio.

Scipione began working from museum biology and anthropology collections at the Smithsonian and other museums in the mid-90s, incorporating the imagery into her artwork. In 2007, she began an ongoing drawing study of human skulls of historic peoples from global, anthropological collections. Her most recent series of works returns to forms from Renaissance paintings as their source.

She is active as an artist and arts organizer in the NY/NJ metropolitan area, managing the Rainbow Thursdays Artists program for developmentally disabled adults and an afterschool art program for special ed. students.

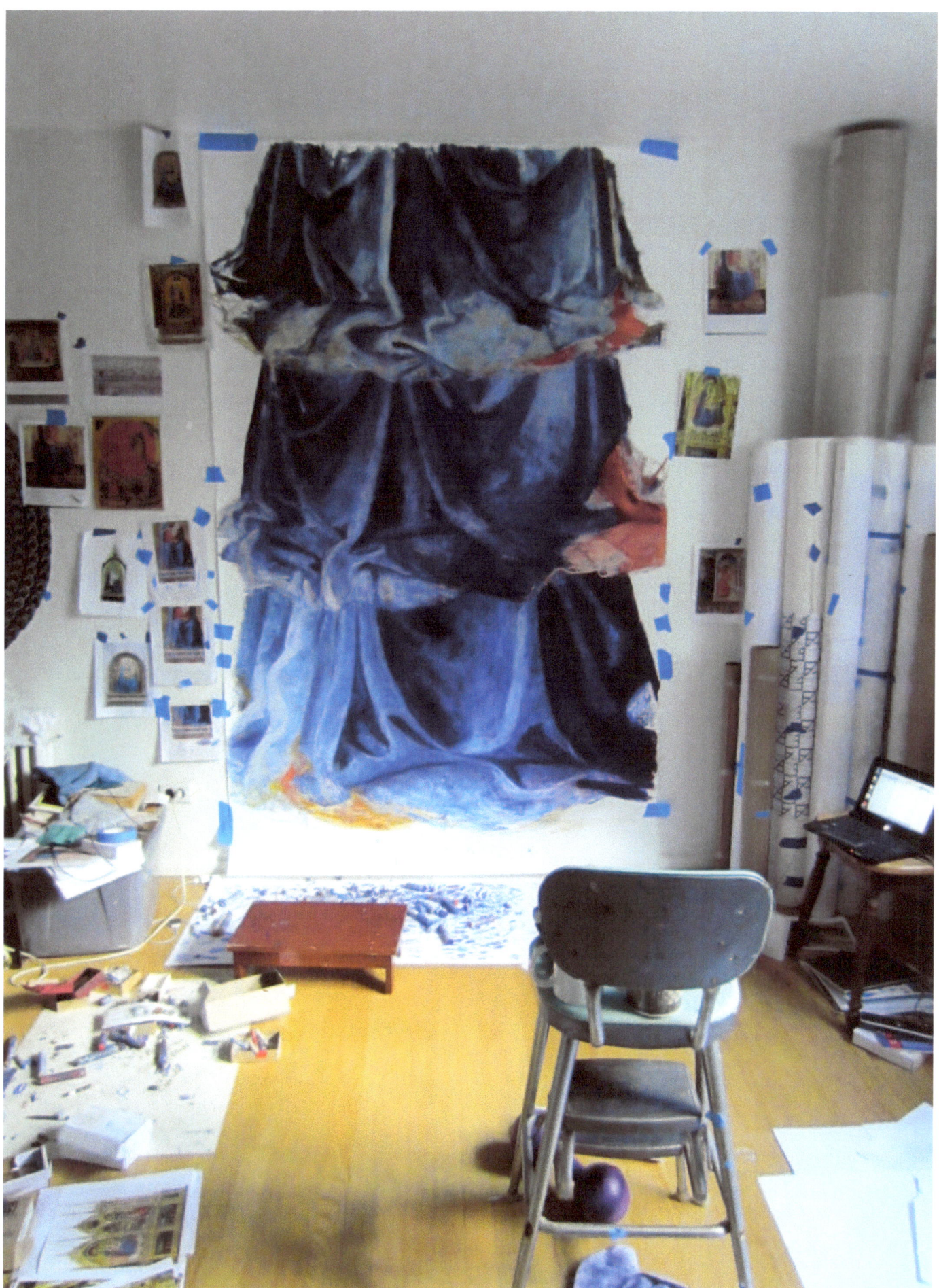

Studio 2014

VICTORY HALL PRESS

is a division of Victory Hall Inc.,
a not-for-profit arts organization producing
exhibitions, events, education programs, public
projects and publications,
based in the NJ/NY metro area.

Other books include:

DRAWING ROOMS

Maria Pavlovska: REACTION- Drawing Cycles 2005 – 2015
Pictures of Everything: Abstract Painting Now
The Big Small Show 2014

PORTRAIT PROJECT

Ross Bonn:100 People
Ian Charles Scott:: The Shape of the Being

NEW DRAWING SERIES

presents series of innovative, current images
from artists whose work explores and expands
the visual and conceptual language of drawing.

Ibou Ndoye: Forms of Faces
Ibou Ndoye: Taarou Adaa
Jill Scipione: Skullnotebook
Carl Vierow: Detective at Red Castle Pier and Other Drawings
James Pustorino: Universechild
Hector G Romero: Last Coast Blues
Cheryl Gross: Drawings from the Z Factor

To order copies : victoryhallpress.org

Victory Hall Inc.
74 W 46 St
Bayonne, NJ 07002
www.victoryhall.org

October 2015
Victory Hall Press
ISBN-13: 978-0692460351
ISBN-10: 0692460357

Copyright © 2015

Editor: James Pustorino
website: www.victoryhallpress.org
contact: victoryhall1@msn.com

This program is made possible in part by funds from the New Jersey State Council on the
Arts/Department of State, a partner agency of the National Endowment for the Arts, administered by
the Hudson County Office of Cultural and Heritage Affairs, Thomas A. Degise, County Executive, and the
Board of Chosen Freeholders.

www.ingramcontent.com/pod-product-compliance
Lightning Source LLC
Chambersburg PA
CBHW050854180526
45159CB00007B/2674